JAPANESE FAIRY WORLD: ST WONDER-LORE OF JAPAN
BY
William Elliot Griffis

JAPANESE FAIRY WORLD: STORIES FROM THE WONDER-LORE OF JAPAN

Published by Mythik Press

New York City, NY

First published circa 1928

Copyright © Mythik Press, 2015

All rights reserved

Except in the United States of America, this book is sold subject to the condition that it shall not, by way of trade or otherwise, be lent, re-sold, hired out, or otherwise circulated without the publisher's prior consent in any form of binding or cover other than that in which it is published and without a similar condition including this condition being imposed on the subsequent purchaser.

ABOUT MYTHIK PRESS

From the moment people first began practicing rituals, they have been creating folk tales and legends to celebrate their past and create a unique cultural identity. **Mythik Press** carries these legacies forward by publishing the greatest stories ever concocted, from King Arthur to the fairy tales of the Brothers Grimm.

JAPANESE FAIRY WORLD.

Stories from the Wonder-lore of Japan.
AUTHOR OF "THE MIKADO'S EMPIRE."
ILLUSTRATED BY OZAWA, OF TOKIO.
LONDON:
TRÜBNER & CO., LUDGATE HILL.
1887.

PREFACE.

The thirty-four stories included within this volume do not illustrate the bloody, revengeful or licentious elements, with which Japanese popular, and juvenile literature is saturated. These have been carefully avoided.

It is also rather with a view to the artistic, than to the literary, products of the imagination of Japan, that the selection has been made. From my first acquaintance, twelve years ago, with Japanese youth, I became an eager listener to their folk lore and fireside stories. When later, during a residence of nearly four years among the people, my eyes were opened to behold the wondrous fertility of invention, the wealth of literary, historic and classic allusion, of pun, myth and riddle, of heroic, wonder, and legendary lore in Japanese art, I at once set myself to find the source of the ideas expressed in bronze and porcelain, on lacquered cabinets, fans, and even crape paper napkins and tidies. Sometimes I discovered the originals of the artist's fancy in books, sometimes only in the mouths of the people and professional story-tellers. Some of these stories I first read on the tattooed limbs and bodies of the native foot-runners, others I first saw in flower-tableaux at the street floral shows of Tokio. Within this book the reader will find translations, condensations of whole books, of interminable romances, and a few sketches by the author embodying Japanese ideas, beliefs and superstitions. I have taken no more liberty, I think, with the native originals, than a modern story-teller of Tokio would himself take, were he talking in an American parlor, instead of at his bamboo-curtained stand in Yanagi Cho, (Willow Street,) in the mikado's capital.

Some of the stories have appeared in English before, but most of them are printed for the first time. A few reappear from The Independent and other periodicals.

The illustrations and cover-stamp, though engraved in New York by Mr. Henry W. Troy, were, with one exception, drawn especially for this work, by my artist-friend, Ozawa Nankoku, of Tokio. The picture of Yorimasa, the Archer, was made for me by one of my students in Tokio.

Hoping that these harmless stories that have tickled the imagination of Japanese children during untold generations, may amuse the big and little folks of America, the writer invites his readers, in the language of the native host as he points to the chopsticks and spread table, O agari nasai

W.E.G.

Schenectady, N.Y., Sept. 28th, 1880.

THE MEETING OF THE STAR-LOVERS.

O
ONE of the greatest days in the calendar of old Japan was the seventh of July; or, as the Japanese people put it, "the seventh day of the seventh month." It was a vermilion day in the almanacs, to which every child looked forward with eyes sparkling, hands clapping, and fingers counting, as each night rolled the time nearer. All manner of fruits and other eatable vegetables were prepared, and cakes baked, in the household. The boys plucked bamboo stalks, and strung on their branches bright-colored ribbons, tinkling bells, and long streamers of paper, on which poetry was written. On this night, mothers hoped for wealth, happiness, good children, and wisdom. The girls made a wish that they might become skilled in needlework. Only one wish a year, however, could be made. So, if any one wanted several things—health, wealth, skill in needlework, wisdom, etc.—they must wait many years before all the favors could be granted. Above all things, rainy weather was not desired. It was a "good sign" when a spider spun his web over a melon, or, if put in a square box he should weave a circular web. Now, the cause of all this preparation was that on the seventh of July the Herd-boy star and the Spinning Maiden star cross the Milky Way to meet each other. These are the stars which we call Capricornus and Alpha Lyra. These stars that shine and glitter so far up in the zenith, are the boy with an ox and the girl with a shuttle, about whom the story runs as follows:

On the banks of the Silver River of Heaven (which we call the Milky Way) there lived a beautiful maiden, who was the daughter of the sun. Her name was Shokujo. She did not care for games or play, like her companions, and, thinking nothing of vain display, wore only the simplest of dress. Yet she was very diligent, and made many garments for others. Indeed, so busy was she that all called her the Weaving or Spinning Princess.

The sun-king noticed the serious disposition and close habits of his daughter, and tried in various ways to get her to be more lively. At last he thought to marry her. As marriages in the star-land are usually planned by the parents, and not by the foolish lover-boys and girls, he arranged the union without consulting his daughter. The young man on whom the sun-king thus bestowed his daughter's hand was Kingin, who kept a herd of cows on the banks of the celestial stream. He had always been a good neighbor, and, living on the same side of the river, the father thought he would get a nice son-in-law, and at the same time improve his daughter's habits and disposition.

No sooner did the maiden become wife than her habits and character utterly changed for the worse, and the father had a very vexatious case of tadashiku suguru ("too much of a good thing") on his hands. The wife became not only very merry and lively, but utterly forsook loom and needle. She gave up her nights and days to play and idleness, and no silly lover could have been more foolish than she.

The sun-king became very much offended at all this, and thinking that the husband was the cause of it, he determined to separate the couple. So he ordered the husband to remove to the other side of the river of stars, and told him that hereafter they should meet only once a year, on the seventh night of the seventh month. To make a bridge over the flood of stars, the sun-king called myriads of magpies, which thereupon flew together, and, making a bridge, supported him on their wings and backs as if it were a roadway of solid land. So, bidding his weeping wife farewell, the lover-husband sorrowfully crossed the River of Heaven. No sooner had he set foot on the opposite side than the magpies flew away, filling all the heavens with their chatter. The weeping wife and lover-husband stood for a long time wistfully gazing at each other from afar. Then they separated, the one to lead his ox, the other to ply her shuttle during the long hours of the day with diligent toil. Thus they filled the hours, and the sun-king again rejoiced in his daughter's industry.

But when night fell, and all the lamps of heaven were lighted, the lovers would come and stand by the banks of the starry river, and gaze longingly at each other, waiting for the seventh night of the seventh month.

At last the time drew near, and only one fear possessed the loving wife. Every time she thought of it her heart played pit-a-pat faster. What if it should rain? For the River of Heaven is always full to the brim, and one extra drop of rain causes a flood which sweeps away even the bird-bridge.

THE STAR-LOVERS MEETING ON THE BRIDGE OF BIRDS.
THE STAR-LOVERS MEETING ON THE BRIDGE OF BIRDS.

But not a drop fell. The seventh month, seventh night, came, and all the heavens were clear. The magpies flew joyfully in myriads, making one way for the tiny feet of the little lady. Trembling with joy, and with heart fluttering more than the bridge of wings, she crossed the River of Heaven, and was in the arms of her husband. This she did every year. The lover-husband stayed on his side of the river, and the wife came to him on the magpie bridge, save on the sad occasion when it rained. So every year the people hope for clear weather, and the happy festival is celebrated alike by old and young.

THE TRAVELS OF TWO FROGS.

F

FORTY miles apart, as the cranes fly, stand the great cities of Ozaka and Kioto. The one is the city of canals and bridges. Its streets are full of bustling trade, and its waterways are ever alive with gondolas, shooting hither and thither like the wooden shuttles in a loom. The other is the sacred city of the Mikado's empire, girdled with green hills and a nine-fold circle of flowers. In its quiet, clean streets, laid out like a chessboard, walk the shaven monks and gowned scholars. And very beautiful is Kioto, with pretty girls, and temple gardens, and castle walls, and towers, and moats in which the white lotus blooms.

Long, long ago, in the good old days before the hairy-faced and pale-cheeked men from over the Sea of Great Peace (Pacific Ocean) came to Japan; before the black coal-smoke and snorting engine scared the white heron from the rice-fields; before black crows and fighting sparrows, which fear not man, perched on telegraph wires, or ever a railway was thought of, there lived two frogs—one in a well in Kioto, the other in a lotus-pond in Ozaka.

Now it is a common proverb in the Land of the Gods (Japan) that "the frog in the well knows not the great ocean," and the Kioto frog had so often heard this scornful sneer from the maids who came to draw out water, with their long bamboo-handled buckets that he resolved to travel abroad and see the world, and especially the tai kai (the great ocean).

"I'll see for myself," said Mr. Frog, as he packed his wallet and wiped his spectacles, "what this great ocean is that they talk about. I'll wager it isn't half as deep or wide as well, where I can see the stars even at daylight."

Now the truth was, a recent earthquake had greatly reduced the depth of the well and the water was getting very shallow. Mr. Frog informed his family of his intentions. Mrs. Frog wept a great deal; but, drying her eyes with her paper handkerchief, she declared she would count the hours on her fingers till he came back, and at every morning and evening meal would set out his table with food on it, just as if he were home. She tied up a little lacquered box full of boiled rice and snails for his journey, wrapped it around with a silk napkin, and, putting his extra clothes in a bundle, swung it on his back. Tying it over his neck, he seized his staff and was ready to go.

"Sayonara" ("Good-bye") cried he, as, with a tear in his eye, he walked away.

"Sayonara. Oshidzukani" ("Good-bye. Walk slowly"), croaked Mrs. Frog and the whole family of young frogs in a chorus.

Two of the froggies were still babies, that is, they were yet polywogs, with a half inch of tail still on them; and, of course, were carried about by being strapped on the back of their older brothers.

Mr. Frog being now on land, out of his well, noticed that the other animals did not leap, but walked on their legs. And, not wishing to be eccentric, he likewise began briskly walking upright on his hind legs or waddling on all fours.

Now it happened that about the same time the Ozaka father frog had become restless and dissatisfied with life on the edges of his lotus-ditch. He had made up his mind to "cast the lion's cub into the valley."

"Why! that is tall talk for a frog, I must say," exclaims the reader. "What did he mean?"

I must tell you that the Ozaka frog was a philosopher. Right at the edge of his lotus-pond was a monastery, full of Buddhist monks, who every day studied their sacred rolls and droned over the books of Confucius, to learn them by heart. Our frog had heard them so often that he could (in frog language, of course) repeat many of their wise sentences and intone responses to their evening prayers put up by the great idol Amida. Indeed, our frog had so often listened to their debates on texts from the classics that he had himself become a sage and a philosopher. Yet, as the proverb says, "the sage is not happy."

Why not? In spite of a soft mud-bank, plenty of green scum, stagnant water, and shady lotus leaves, a fat wife and a numerous family; in short, everything to make a frog happy, his forehead, or rather gullet, was wrinkled with care from long pondering of knotty problems, such as the following:

The monks often come down to the edge of the pond to look at the pink and white lotus. One summer day, as a little frog, hardly out of his tadpole state, with a small fragment of tail still left, sat basking on a huge round leaf, one monk said to the other:

"Of what does that remind you?"

"The babies of frogs will become but frogs," said one shaven pate, laughing.

"What think you?"

"The white lotus flower springs out of the black mud," said the other, solemnly, as both walked away.

The old frog, sitting near by, overheard them and began to philosophize: "Humph! The babies of frogs will become but frogs, hey? If mud becomes lotus, why shouldn't a frog become a man? Why not? If my pet son should travel abroad and see the world—go to Kioto, for instance—why shouldn't he be as wise as those shining-headed men, I wonder? I shall try it, anyhow. I'll send my son on a journey to Kioto. I'll 'cast the lion's cub into the valley' (send the pet son abroad in the world, to see and study) at once. I'll deny myself for the sake of my offspring."

Flump! splash! sounded the water, as a pair of webby feet disappeared. The "lion's cub" was soon ready, after much paternal advice, and much counsel to beware of being gobbled up by long-legged storks, and trod on by impolite men, and struck at by bad boys. "Kio ni no inaka" ("Even in the capital there are boors") said Father Frog.

Now it so happened that the old frog from Kioto and the "lion's cub" from Ozaka started each from his home at the same time. Nothing of importance occurred to either of them until, as luck would have it, they met on a hill near Hashimoto, which is half way between the two cities. Both were footsore, and websore, and very tired, especially about the hips, on account of the unfroglike manner of walking, instead of hopping, as they had been used to.

"Ohio gozarimasu" ("Good-morning") said the "lion's cub" to the old frog, as he fell on all fours and bowed his head to the ground three times, squinting up over his left eye, to see if the other frog was paying equal deference in return.

"He, konnichi wa" ("Yes, good-day") replied the Kioto frog.

"O tenki" ("It is rather fine weather to-day") said the "cub."

"He, yoi tenki gozence" ("Yes, it is very fine") replied the old fellow.

"I am Gamataro, from Ozaka, the oldest son of Hiki Dono, Sensui no Kami" (Lord Bullfrog, Prince of the Lotus-Ditch).

"Your Lordship must be weary with your journey. I am Kayeru San of Idomidzu (Sir Frog of the Well) in Kioto. I started out to see the 'great ocean' from Ozaka; but, I declare, my hips are so dreadfully tired that I believe that I'll give up my plan and content myself with a look from this hill."

The truth must be owned that the old frog was not only on his hind legs, but also on his last legs, when he stood up to look at Ozaka; while the "cub" was tired enough to believe anything. The old fellow, wiping his face, spoke up:

"Suppose we save ourselves the trouble of the journey. This hill is half way between the two cities, and while I see Ozaka and the sea you can get a good look of the Kio" (Capital, or Kioto).

"Happy thought!" said the Ozaka frog.

Then both reared themselves upon their hind-legs, and stretching upon their toes, body to body, and neck to neck, propped each other up, rolled their goggles and looked steadily, as they supposed, on the places which they each wished to see. Now everyone knows that a frog has eyes mounted in that part of his head which is front when he is down and back when he stands up. They are set like a compass on gimbals.

Long and steadily they gazed, until, at last, their toes being tired, they fell down on all fours.

"I declare!" said the old yaze (daddy) "Ozaka looks just like Kioto; and as for 'the great ocean' those stupid maids talked about, I don't see any at all, unless they mean that strip of river that looks for all the world like the Yodo. I don't believe there is any 'great ocean'!"

"As for my part," said the 'cub', "I am satisfied that it's all folly to go further; for Kioto is as like Ozaka as one grain of rice is like another." Then he said to himself: "Old Totsu San (my father) is a fool, with all his philosophy."

Thereupon both congratulated themselves upon the happy labor-saving expedient by which they had spared themselves a long journey, much leg-weariness, and some danger. They departed, after exchanging many compliments; and, dropping again into a frog's hop, they leaped back in half the time—the one to his well and the other to his pond. There each told the story of both cities looking exactly alike; thus demonstrating the folly of those foolish folks called men. As for the old gentleman in the lotus-pond, he was so glad to get the "cub" back again that he never again tried to reason out the problems of philosophy. And to this day the frog in the well knows not and believes not in the "great ocean." Still do the babies of frogs become but frogs. Still is it vain to teach the reptiles philosophy; for all such labor is "like pouring water in a frog's face." Still out of the black mud springs the glorious white lotus in celestial purity, unfolding its stainless petals to the smiling heavens, the emblem of life and resurrection.

THE CHILD OF THE THUNDER.

I

IN among the hills of Echizen, within sight of the snowy mountain called Hakuzan, lived a farmer named Bimbo. He was very poor, but frugal and industrious. He was very fond of children though he had none himself. He longed to adopt a son to bear his name, and often talked the matter over with his old dame. But being so dreadfully poor both thought it best not to adopt, until they had bettered their condition and increased the area of their land. For all the property Bimbo owned was the earth in a little gully, which he himself was reclaiming. A tiny rivulet, flowing from a spring in the crevice of the rocks above, after trickling over the boulders, rolled down the gully to join a brook in the larger valley below. Bimbo had with great labor, after many years, made dams or terraces of stone, inside which he had thrown soil, partly got from the mountain sides, but mainly carried in baskets on the backs of himself and his wife, from the valley below. By such weary toil, continued year in and year out, small beds of soil were formed, in which rice could be planted and grown. The little rivulet supplied the needful water; for rice, the daily food of laborer and farmer, must be planted and cultivated in soft mud under water. So the little rivulet, which once leaped over the rock and cut its way singing to the valley, now spread itself quietly over each terrace, making more than a dozen descents before it reached the fields below.

Yet after all his toil for a score of years, working every day from the first croak of the raven, until the stars came out, Bimbo and his wife owned only three tan (¾ acre) of terrace land. Sometimes a summer would pass, and little or no rain fall. Then the rivulet dried up and crops failed. It seemed all in vain that their backs were bent and their foreheads seamed and wrinkled with care. Many a time did Bimbo have hard work of it even to pay his taxes, which sometimes amounted to half his crop. Many a time did he shake his head, muttering the discouraged farmer's proverb "A new field gives a scant crop," the words of which mean also, "Human life is but fifty years."

One summer day after a long drought, when the young rice sprouts, just transplanted were turning yellow at the tips, the clouds began to gather and roll, and soon a smart shower fell, the lightning glittered, and the hills echoed with claps of thunder. But Bimbo, hoe in hand, was so glad to see the rain fall, and the pattering drops felt so cool and refreshing, that he worked on, strengthening the terrace to resist the little flood about to come.

Pretty soon the storm rattled very near him, and he thought he had better seek shelter, lest the thunder should strike and kill him. For Bimbo, like all his neighbors, had often heard stories of Kaijin, the god of the thunder-drums, who lives in the skies and rides on the storm, and sometimes kills people by throwing out of the clouds at them a terrible creature like a cat, with iron-like claws and a hairy body.

Just as Bimbo threw his hoe over his shoulder and started to move, a terrible blinding flash of lightning dazzled his eyes. It was immediately followed by a deafening crash, and the thunder fell just in front of him. He covered his eyes with his hands, but finding himself unhurt, uttered a prayer of thanks to Buddha for safety. Then he uncovered his eyes and looked down at his feet.

There lay a little boy, rosy and warm, and crowing in the most lively manner, and never minding the rain in the least. The farmer's eyes opened very wide, but happy and nearly surprised out of his senses, he picked up the child tenderly in his arms, and took him home to his old wife.

"Here's a gift from Raijin," said Bimbo. "We'll adopt him as our own son and call him Raitaro," (the first-born darling of the thunder).

So the boy grew up and became a very dutiful and loving child. He was as kind and obedient to his foster-parents as though he had been born in their house. He never liked to play with other children, but kept all day in the fields with his father, sporting with the rivulet and looking at the clouds and sky. Even when the strolling players of the Dai Kagura (the comedy which makes the gods laugh) and the "Lion of Corea" came into the village, and every boy and girl and nurse and woman was sure to be out in great glee, the child of the thunder stayed up in the field, or climbed on the high rocks to watch the sailing of the birds and the flowing of the water and the river far away.

Great prosperity seemed to come to the farmer, and he laid it all to the sweet child that fell to him from the clouds. It was very curious that rain often fell on Bimbo's field when none fell elsewhere; so that Bimbo grew rich and changed his name to Kanemochi. He believed that the boy Raitaro beckoned to the clouds, and they shed their rain for him.

A good many summers passed by, and Raitaro had grown to be a tall and handsome lad, almost a man and eighteen years old. On his birthday the old farmer and the good wife made a little feast for their foster-child. They ate and drank and talked of the thunder-storm, out of which Raitaro was born.

Finally the young man said solemnly:

"My dear parents, I thank you very much for your kindness to me, but I must now say farewell. I hope you will always be happy."

Then, in a moment, all trace of a human form disappeared, and floating in the air, they saw a tiny white dragon, which hovered for a moment above them, and then flew away. The old couple went out of doors to watch it, when it grew bigger and bigger, taking its course to the hills above, where the piled-up white clouds, which form on a summer's afternoon, seemed built up like towers and castles of silver. Towards one of these the dragon moved, until, as they watched his form, now grown to a mighty size, it disappeared from view.

After this Kanemochi and his wife, who were now old and white-headed, ceased from their toil and lived in comfort all their days. When they died and their bodies were reduced to a heap of white cinders in the stone furnace of the village cremation-house, their ashes were mixed, and being put into one urn, were laid away in the cemetery of the temple yard. Their tomb was carved in the form of a white dragon, which to this day, in spite of mosses and lichens, may still be seen among the ancient monuments of the little hamlet.

THE TONGUE-CUT SPARROW.

THERE was once an old man who had a wife with a very bad temper. She had never borne him any children, and would not take the trouble to adopt a son. So for a little pet he kept a tiny sparrow, and fed it with great care. The old dame not satisfied with scolding her husband hated the sparrow.

Now the old woman's temper was especially bad on wash days, when her old back and knees were well strained over the low tub, which rested on the ground.

It happened once that she had made some starch, and set it in a red wooden bowl to cool. While her back was turned, the sparrow hopped down on the edge of the bowl, and pecked at some of the starch. In a rage the old hag seized a pair of scissors and cut the sparrow's tongue out. Flinging the bird in the air she cried out, "Now be off." So the poor sparrow, all bleeding, flew away.

When the old man came back and found his pet gone, he made a great ado. He asked his wife, and she told him what she had done and why. The sorrowful old man grieved sorely for his pet, and after looking in every place and calling it by name, gave it up as lost.

Long after this, old man while wandering on the mountains met his old friend the sparrow. They both cried "Ohio!" (good morning,) to each other, and bowing low offered many mutual congratulations and inquiries as to health, etc. Then the sparrow begged the old man to visit his humble abode, promising to introduce his wife and two daughters.

The old man went in and found a nice little house with a bamboo garden, tiny waterfall, stepping stone and everything complete. Then Mrs. Sparrow brought in slices of sugar-jelly, rock-candy, sweet potato custard, and a bowl of hot starch sprinkled with sugar, and a pair of chopsticks on a tray. Miss Suzumi, the elder daughter brought the tea caddy and tea-pot, and in a snap of the fingers had a good cup of tea ready, which she offered on a tray, kneeling.

"Please take up and help yourself. The refreshments are very poor, but I hope you will excuse our plainness," said Mother Sparrow. The delighted old man, wondering in himself at such a polite family of sparrows, ate heartily, and drank several cups of tea. Finally, on being pressed he remained all night.

For several days the old man enjoyed himself at the sparrow's home. He looked at the landscapes and the moonlight, feasted to his heart's content, and played go (the game of 360 checkers) with Ko-suzumi the little daughter. In the evening Mrs. Sparrow would bring out the refreshments and the wine, and seat the old man on a silken cushion, while she played the guitar. Mr. Sparrow and his two daughters danced, sung and made merry. The delighted old man leaning on the velvet arm-rest forgot his cares, his old limbs and his wife's tongue, and felt like a youth again.

On the fifth day the old man said he must go home. Then the sparrow brought out two baskets made of plaited rattan, such as are used in traveling and carried on men's shoulders. Placing them before their guest, the sparrow said, "Please accept a parting gift."

Now one basket was very heavy, and the other very light. The old man, not being greedy, said he would take the lighter one. So with many thanks and bows and good-byes, he set off homewards.

He reached his hut safely, but instead of a kind welcome the old hag began to scold him for being away so long. He begged her to be quiet, and telling of his visit to the sparrows, opened the basket, while the scowling old woman held her tongue, out of sheer curiosity.

Oh, what a splendid sight! There were gold and silver coin, and gems, and coral, and crystal, and amber, and the never-failing bag of money, and the invisible coat and hat, and rolls of books, and all manner of precious things.

At the sight of so much wealth, the old hag's scowl changed to a smile of greedy joy. "I'll go right off and get a present from the sparrows," said she.

So binding on her straw sandals, and tucking up her skirts, and adjusting her girdle, tying the bow in front, she seized her staff and set off on the road. Arriving at the sparrow's house she began to flatter Mr. Sparrow by soft speeches. Of course the polite sparrow invited her into his house, but nothing but a cup of tea was offered her, and wife and daughters kept away. Seeing she was not going to get any good-bye gift, the brazen hussy asked for one. The sparrow then brought out and set before her two baskets, one heavy and the other light. Taking the heavier one without so much as saying "thank you," she carried it back with her. Then she opened it, expecting all kinds of riches.

She took off the lid, when a horrible cuttle-fish rushed at her, and a horned oni snapped his tusks at her, a skeleton poked his bony fingers in her face, and finally a long, hairy serpent, with a big head and lolling tongue, sprang out and coiled around her, cracking her bones, and squeezing out her breath, till she died.

After the good old man had buried his wife, he adopted a son to comfort his old age, and with his treasures lived at ease all his days.

THE FIRE-FLY'S LOVERS.

I

IN JAPAN the night-flies emit so brilliant a light and are so beautiful that ladies go out in the evenings and catch the insects for amusement, as may be seen represented on Japanese fans. They imprison them in tiny cages made of bamboo threads, and hang them up in their rooms or suspend them from the eaves of their houses. At their picnic parties, the people love to sit on August evenings, fan in hand, looking over the lovely landscape, spangled by ten thousand brilliant spots of golden light. Each flash seems like a tiny blaze of harmless lightning.

One of the species of night-flies, the most beautiful of all, is a source of much amusement to the ladies. Hanging the cage of glittering insects on their verandahs, they sit and watch the crowd of winged visitors attracted by the fire-fly's light. What brings them there, and why the fire-fly's parlor is filled with suitors as a queen's court with courtiers, let this love story tell.

On the southern and sunny side of the castle moats of the Fukui castle, in Echizen, the water had long ago become shallow so that lotus lilies grew luxuriantly. Deep in the heart of one of the great flowers whose petals were as pink as the lining of a sea-shell, lived the King of the Fire-flies, Hi-ō, whose only daughter was the lovely princess Hotaru-himé. While still a child the himé (princess) was carefully kept at home within the pink petals of the lily, never going even to the edges except to see her father fly off on his journey. Dutifully she waited until of age, when the fire glowed in her own body, and shone, beautifully illuminating the lotus, until its light at night was like a lamp within a globe of coral.

Every night her light grew brighter and brighter, until at last it was as mellow as gold. Then her father said:

"My daughter is now of age, she may fly abroad with me sometimes, and when the proper suitor comes she may marry whom she will."

So Hotaru-himé flew forth in and out among the lotus lilies of the moat, then into rich rice fields, and at last far off to the indigo meadows.

Whenever she went a crowd of suitors followed her, for she had the singular power of attracting all the night-flying insects to herself. But she cared for none of their attentions, and though she spoke politely to them all she gave encouragement to none. Yet some of the sheeny-winged gallants called her a coquette.

One night she said to her mother, the queen:

"I have met many admirers, but I don't wish a husband from any of them. Tonight I shall stay at home, and if any of them love me truly they will come and pay me court here. Then I shall lay an impossible duty on them. If they are wise they will not try to perform it; and if they love their lives more than they love me, I do not want any of them. Whoever succeeds may have me for his bride."

"As you will my child," said the queen mother, who arrayed her daughter in her most resplendent robes, and set her on her throne in the heart of the lotus.

Then she gave orders to her body-guard to keep all suitors at a respectful distance lest some stupid gallant, a horn-bug or a cockchafer dazzled by the light should approach too near and hurt the princess or shake her throne.

No sooner had twilight faded away, than forth came the golden beetle, who stood on a stamen and making obeisance, said:—

"I am Lord Green-Gold, I offer my house, my fortune and my love to Princess Hotaru."

"Go and bring me fire and I will be your bride" said Hotaru-himé.

With a bow of the head the beetle opened his wings and departed with a stately whirr.

Next came a shining bug with wings and body as black as lamp-smoke, who solemnly professed his passion.

"Bring me fire and you may have me for your wife."

Off flew the bug with a buzz.

Pretty soon came the scarlet dragon-fly, expecting so to dazzle the princess by his gorgeous colors that she would accept him at once.

"I decline your offer" said the princess, "but if you bring me a flash of fire, I'll become your bride."

Swift was the flight of the dragon-fly on his errand, and in came the Beetle with a tremendous buzz, and ardently plead his suit.

"I'll say 'yes' if you bring me fire" said the glittering princess.

Suitor after suitor appeared to woo the daughter of the King of the Fire-flies until every petal was dotted with them. One after another in a long troop they appeared. Each in his own way, proudly, humbly, boldly, mildly, with flattery, with boasting, even with tears, each proffered his love, told his rank or expatiated on his fortune or vowed his constancy, sang his tune or played his music. To every one of her lovers the princess in modest voice returned the same answer:

"Bring me fire and I'll be your bride."

So without telling his rivals, each one thinking he had the secret alone sped away after fire.

But none ever came back to wed the princess. Alas for the poor suitors! The beetle whizzed off to a house near by through the paper windows of which light glimmered. So full was he of his passion that thinking nothing of wood or iron, he dashed his head against a nail, and fell dead on the ground.

The black bug flew into a room where a poor student was reading. His lamp was only a dish of earthenware full of rape seed oil with a wick made of pith. Knowing nothing of oil the love-lorn bug crawled into the dish to reach the flame and in a few seconds was drowned in the oil.

"Nan jaro?" (What's that?) said a thrifty housewife, sitting with needle in hand, as her lamp flared up for a moment, smoking the chimney, and then cracking it; while picking out the scorched bits she found a roasted dragon-fly, whose scarlet wings were all burned off.

Mad with love the brilliant hawk-moth, afraid of the flame yet determined to win the fire for the princess, hovered round and round the candle flame, coming nearer and nearer each time. "Now or never, the princess or death," he buzzed, as he darted forward to snatch a flash of flame, but singeing his wings, he fell helplessly down, and died in agony.

"What a fool he was, to be sure," said the ugly clothes moth, coming on the spot, "I'll get the fire. I'll crawl up inside the candle." So he climbed up the hollow paper wick, and was nearly to the top, and inside the hollow blue part of the flame, when the man, snuffing the wick, crushed him to death.

Sad indeed was the fate of the lovers of Hi-ō's daughter. Some hovered around the beacons on the headland, some fluttered about the great wax candles which stood eight feet high in their brass sockets in Buddhist temples; some burned their noses at the top of incense sticks, or were nearly choked by the smoke; some danced all night around the lanterns in the shrines; some sought the sepulchral lamps in the graveyard; one visited the cremation furnace; another the kitchen, where a feast was going on; another chased the sparks that flew out of the chimney; but none brought fire to the princess, or won the lover's prize. Many lost their feelers, had their shining bodies scorched or their wings singed, but most of them alas! lay dead, black and cold next morning.

As the priests trimmed the lamps in the shrines, and the servant maids the lanterns, each said alike:

"The Princess Hotaru must have had many lovers last night."

Alas! alas! poor suitors. Some tried to snatch a streak of green fire from the cat's eyes, and were snapped up for their pains. One attempted to get a mouthful of bird's breath, but was swallowed alive. A carrion beetle (the ugly lover) crawled off to the sea shore, and found some fish scales that emitted light. The stag-beetle climbed a mountain, and in a rotten tree stump found some bits of glowing wood like fire, but the distance was so great that long before they reached the castle moat it was daylight, and the fire had gone out; so they threw their fish scales and old wood away.

The next day was one of great mourning and there were so many funerals going on, that Hi-marō the Prince of the Fire-flies on the north side of the castle moat inquired of his servants the cause. Then he learned for the first time of the glittering princess. Upon this the prince who had just succeeded his father upon the throne fell in love with the princess and resolved to marry her. He sent his chamberlain to ask of her father his daughter in marriage according to true etiquette. The father agreed to the prince's proposal, with the condition that the Prince should obey her behest in one thing, which was to come in person bringing her fire.

Then the Prince at the head of his glittering battalions came in person and filled the lotus palace with a flood of golden light. But Hotaru-himé was so beautiful that her charms paled not their fire even in the blaze of the Prince's glory. The visit ended in wooing, and the wooing in wedding. On the night appointed, in a palanquin made of the white lotus-petals, amid the blazing torches of the prince's battalions of warriors, Hotaru-himé was borne to the prince's palace and there, prince and princess were joined in the wedlock.

Many generations have passed since Hi-marō and Hotaru-himé were married, and still it is the whim of all Fire-fly princesses that their base-born lovers must bring fire as their love-offering or lose their prize. Else would the glittering fair ones be wearied unto death by the importunity of their lovers. Great indeed is the loss, for in this quest of fire many thousand insects, attracted by the fire-fly, are burned to death in the vain hope of winning the fire that shall gain the cruel but beautiful one that fascinates them. It is for this cause that each night insects hover around the lamp flame, and every morning a crowd of victims drowned in the oil, or scorched in the flame, must be cleaned from the lamp. This is the reason why young ladies catch and imprison the fire-flies to watch the war of insect-love, in the hope that they may have human lovers who will dare as much, through fire and flood, as they.

THE BATTLE OF THE APE AND THE CRAB.

I

IN THE LAND where neither the monkeys or the cats have tails, and the persimmons grow to be as large as apples and with seeds bigger than a melon's, there once lived a land crab in the side of a sand hill. One day an ape came along having a persimmon seed, which he offered to swap with the crab for a rice-cake. The crab agreed, and planting the seed in his garden went out every day to watch it grow.

By-and-by the ape came to visit the crab, and seeing the fine tree laden with the yellow-brown fruit, begged a few. The crab, asking pardon of the ape, said he could not climb the tree to offer him any, but agreed to give the ape half, if he would mount the tree and pluck them.

So the monkey ran up the tree, while the crab waited below, expecting to eat the ripe fruit. But the monkey sitting on a limb first filled his pockets full, and then picking off all the best ones, greedily ate the pulp, and threw the skin and stones in the crab's face. Every once in a while, he would pull off a green sour persimmon and hit the crab hard, until his shell was nearly cracked. At last the crab thought he would get the best of the ape. So when his enemy had eaten his fill until he was bulged out, he cried out,

"Now Mister Ape, I dare you to come down head-foremost. You can't do it."

So the ape began to descend, head downward. This was just what the crab wanted, for all the finest persimmons rolled out of his pockets on the ground. The crab quickly gathered them up, and with both arms full ran off to his hole. Then the ape was very angry. He kindled a fire, and blew the smoke down the hole, until the crab was nearly choked. The poor crab to save his life had to crawl out.

Then the monkey beat him soundly, and left him for dead.

The crab had not been long thus, when three travelers, a rice-mortar, an egg, and a wasp found him lying on the ground. They carried him into the house, bound up his wounds and while he lay in bed they planned how they might destroy the ape. They all talked of the matter over their cups of tea, and after the mortar had smoked several pipes of tobacco, a plan was agreed on.

So taking the crab along, stiff and sore as he was, they marched to the monkey's castle. The wasp flew inside, and found that their enemy was away from home. Then all entered and hid themselves. The egg cuddled up under the ashes in the hearth. The wasp flew into the closet. The mortar hid behind the door. They then waited for the ape to come home. The crab sat beside the fire.

Towards evening the monkey arrived, and throwing off his coat (which was just what the wasp wanted) he lighted a sulphur match, and kindling a fire, hung on the kettle for a cup of tea, and pulled out his pipe for a smoke. Just as he sat down by the hearth to salute the crab, the egg burst and the hot yolk flew all over him and in his eye, nearly blinding him. He rushed out to the bathroom to plunge in the tub of cold water, when the wasp flew at him and stung his nose. Slipping down, he fell flat on the floor, when the mortar rolled on him and crushed him to death. Then the whole party congratulated the crab on their victory. Grateful for the friendship thus shown, the whole party, crab, mortar and wasp lived in peace together.

The crab married the daughter of a rich crab that lived over the hill, and a great feast of persimmons was spread before the bride's relatives who came to see the ceremony. By-and-by a little crab was born which became a great pet with the mortar and wasp. With no more apes to plague them, they lived very happily.

THE EGG, WASP AND MORTAR ATTACK THE MONKEY.
THE EGG, WASP AND MORTAR ATTACK THE MONKEY.

THE WONDERFUL TEA-KETTLE.

A
A LONG TIME AGO there was an old priest who lived in the temple of Morinji in the province of Hitachi. He cooked his own rice, boiled his own tea, swept his own floor and lived frugally as an honest priest should do.

One day he was sitting near the square fire-place in the middle of the floor. A rope and chain to hold the pot and kettle hung down from the covered hole in the ceiling which did duty as a chimney. A pair of brass tongs was stuck in the ashes and the fire blazed merrily. At the side of the fire-place, on the floor, was a tray filled with tiny tea-cups, a pewter tea-caddy, a bamboo tea-stirrer, and a little dipper. The priest having finished sweeping the ashes off the edges of the hearth with a little whisk of hawk's feathers, was just about to put on the tea when "suzz," "suzz," sang the tea-kettle spout; and then "pattari"—"pattari" said the lid, as it flapped up and down, and the kettle swung backwards and forwards.

"What does this mean?" said the old bonze. "Naru hodo," said he, with a start as the spout of the kettle turned into a badger's nose with its big whiskers, while from the other side sprouted out a long bushy tail.

"Yohodo medzurashi," shouted the priest dropping the tea-caddy and spilling the green tea all over the matting as four hairy legs appeared under the kettle, and the strange compound, half badger and half kettle, jumped off the fire, and began running around the room. To the priest's horror it leaped on a shelf, puffed out its belly and began to beat a tune with its fore-paws as if it were a drum. The old bonze's pupils, hearing the racket rushed in, and after a lively chase, upsetting piles of books and breaking some of the tea-cups, secured the badger, and squeezed him in a keg used for storing the pickled radishes called daikon, (or Japanese sauer-kraut.) They fastened down the lid with a heavy stone. They were sure that the strong odor of the radishes would kill the beast, for no man could possibly survive such a smell, and it was not likely a badger could.

The next morning the tinker of the village called in and the priest told him about his strange visitor. Wishing to show him the animal, he cautiously lifted the lid of the cask, lest the badger, might after all, be still alive, in spite of the stench of the sour mess, when lo! there was nothing but the old iron tea-kettle. Fearing that the utensil might play the same prank again, the priest was glad to sell it to the tinker who bought the kettle for a few iron cash. He carried it to his junk shop, though he thought it felt unusually heavy.

The tinker went to bed as usual that night with his andon, or paper shaded lamp, just back of his head. About midnight, hearing a strange noise like the flapping up and down of an iron pot-lid, he sat up in bed, rubbed his eyes, and there was the iron pot covered with fur and sprouting out legs. In short, it was turning into a hairy beast. Going over to the recess and taking a fan from the rack, the badger climbed up on the frame of the lamp, and began to dance on its one hind leg, waving the fan with its fore-paw. It played many other tricks, until the man started up, and then the badger turned into a tea-kettle again.

"I declare," said the tinker as he woke up next morning, and talked the matter over with his wife. "I'll just 'raise a mountain'" (earn my fortune) on this kettle. It certainly is a very highly accomplished tea-kettle I'll call it the Bumbuku Chagama (The Tea-Kettle accomplished in literature and military art) and exhibit it to the public.

So the tinker hired a professional show-man for his business agent, and built a little theatre and stage. Then he gave an order to a friend of his, an artist, to paint scenery, with Fuji yama and cranes flying in the air, and a crimson sun shining through the bamboo, and a red moon rising over the waves, and golden clouds and tortoises, and the Sumiyoshi couple, and the grasshopper's picnic, and the Procession of Lord Long-legs, and such like. Then he stretched a tight rope of rice-straw across the stage, and the handbills being stuck up in all the barber shops in town, and wooden tickets branded with "Accomplished and Lucky Tea-Kettle Performance, Admit one,"—the show was opened. The house was full and the people came in parties bringing their tea-pots full of tea and picnic boxes full of rice and eggs, and dumplings, made of millet meal, sugared roast-pea cakes, and other refreshments; because they came to stay all day. Mothers brought their babies with them for the children enjoyed it most of all.

Then the tinker, dressed up in his wide ceremonial clothes, with a big fan in his hand, came out on the platform, made his bow and set the wonderful tea-kettle on the stage. Then at a wave of his fan, the kettle ran around on four legs, half badger and half iron, clanking its lid and wagging its tail. Next it turned into a badger, swelled out its body and beat a tune on it like a drum. It danced a jig on the tight rope, and walked the slack rope, holding a fan, or an umbrella in his paw, stood on his head, and finally at a flourish of his master's fan became a cold and rusty tea-kettle again. The audience were wild with delight, and as the fame of the wonderful tea-kettle spread, many people came from great distances.

Year after year the tinker exhibited the wonder until he grew immensely rich. Then he retired from the show business, and out of gratitude took the old kettle to the temple again and deposited it there as a precious relic. It was then named Bumbuku Dai Mio Jin (The Great Illustrious, Accomplished in Literature and the Military Art).

PEACH-PRINCE, AND THE TREASURE ISLAND.

V

VERY LONG, LONG AGO, there lived an old man and woman in a village near a mountain, from which flowed a stream of purest water. This old couple loved each other so dearly and lived together so happily, that the neighbors called them oshi-dori fu-fu (a love-bird couple), after the mandarin ducks which always dwell together in pairs, and are so affectionate that they are said to pine and die if one be taken from the other. The old man was a woodcutter, and the old woman kept house, but they were very lonely for they had no child, and often grieved over their hard lot.

One day while the man was out on the mountain cutting brush, his old crone took her shallow tub and clothes down to the brook to wash. She had not yet begun, when she saw a peach floating with its stem and two leaves in the stream. She picked up the fruit and set it aside to take home and share it with her old man. When he returned she set it before him, not dreaming what was in it. He was just about to cut it open, when the peach fell in half, and there lay a little baby boy. The happy old couple rejoiced over him and reared him tenderly. Because he was their first child (taro) and born of a peach (momo) they called him Momotarō or Peach-Darling.

The most wonderful thing in the child, was his great strength! Even when still a baby, he would astonish his foster-mother by standing on the mats, and lifting her wash tub, or kettle of hot tea, which he would balance above his head without spilling a drop. The little fellow grew to be strong and brave and good. He was always kind to his parents and saved them many a step and much toil. He practiced archery, wrestling, and handling the iron club, until he was not afraid of anybody or anything. He even laughed at the oni, who, were demons living in the clouds or on lonely islands in the sea. Momotarō was also very kind to birds and animals, so that they were very tame, and became his friends, knew him and called him by name.

Now there was an island far out in the ocean, inhabited by onis with horns in their heads, and big sharp tusks in their mouths, who ravaged the shores of Japan and ate up the people. In the centre of the island was the giant Oni's castle, built inside a great cave which was full of all kinds of treasures such as every one wants. These are:

1. The hat which makes the one who puts it on invisible. It looks just like a straw hat, but has a tuft of fine grass on the top, and a pink fringe like the lining of shells, around the brim.

2. A coat like a farmer's grass rain-cloak, which makes the wearer invisible.

3. The crystal jewels which flash fire, and govern the ebb and flow of the tide.

4. Shippō, or "the seven jewels," namely gold and silver, branch of red coral, agate, emerald, crystal and pearl. All together called takare mono, or precious treasures.

Momotaro made up his mind to conquer these demons, and get their treasures. He prepared his weapons and asked the old woman to make him some millet dumplings. So the old lady ground the millet seeds into meal, the old man kneaded the dough, and both made the dumplings which the little hero carefully stuck on skewers and stowed away in a bamboo basket-box. This he wrapped in a silk napkin, and flung it over his shoulder. Seizing his iron club he stuck his flag in his back as the sign of war. The flag was of white silk, crossed by two black bars at the top, and underneath these, was embroidered the device of a peach with a stem and two leaves floating on a running stream. This was his crest or sashimono (banneret). Then he bade the old folks good-bye and walked off briskly. He took his little dog with him, giving him a millet dumpling now and then.

As he passed along he met a monkey chattering and showing his teeth. The monkey said, "Where are you going, Mr. Peach-Darling?"

"I'm going to the oni's island to get his treasures."

"What have you got good in your package?"

"Millet dumplings. Have one?"

"Yes, give me one, and I'll go with you," said the monkey.

So the monkey ate the dumpling, and boy, dog and monkey all trudged on together. A little further on a pheasant met them and said:

"Ohio, Momotarō, doko?" (Good morning, Mr. Peach-Prince, where are you going?). Peach-Prince told him, and at the same time offered him a dumpling. This made the pheasant his friend.

Peach-Prince and his little army of three retainers journeyed on until they reached the sea-shore. There they found a big boat into which Peach-Prince with the dog and monkey embarked, while the pheasant flew over to the island to find a safe place to land, so as to take the onis by surprise.

They quietly reached the door of the cave, and then Momotarō beat in the gate with his iron club. Rushing into the castle, he put the small onis to flight, and dashing forward, the little hero would nearly have reached the room where the giant oni was just waking up after a nights' drunkenness. With a terrible roar he advanced to gobble up Peach-Prince, when the dog ran behind and bit the oni in the leg. The monkey climbed up his back and blinded him with his paws while the pheasant flew in his face. Then Peach-Prince beat him with his iron club, until he begged for his life and promised to give up all his treasures.

The onis brought all their precious things out of the storehouse and laid them on great tables or trays before the little hero and his little army.

Momotaro sat on a rock, with his little army of three retainers around him, holding his fan, with his hands akimbo on his knees, just as mighty generals do after a battle, when they receive the submission of their enemies. On his right sat kneeling on the ground his faithful monkey, while the pheasant and dog sat on the left.

After the onis had surrendered all, they fell down on their hands and knees with their faces in the dust, and acknowledged Peach-Prince as their master, and swore they would ever henceforth be his slaves. Then Peach-Prince, with a wave of his fan bade them rise up and carry the treasures to the largest ship they had, and to point the prow to the land. This done, Momotaro and his company got on board, and the onis bowed farewell.

A stiff breeze sprang up and sent the ship plowing through the waters, and bent out the great white sail like a bow. On the prow was a long black tassel like the mane of a horse, that at every lurch dipped in the waves, and as it rose flung off the spray.

The old couple becoming anxious after their Peach-Darling, had traveled down to the sea shore, and arrived just as the treasure ship hove in sight. Oh how beautiful it looked with its branches of red coral, and shining heaps of gold and silver, and the invisible coat and hat, the dazzling sheen of the jewels of the ebbing and the flowing tide, the glistening pearls, and piles of agate and crystal.

THE ONI SUBMITTING TO PEACH PRINCE.
THE ONI SUBMITTING TO PEACH PRINCE.

Momotaro came home laden with riches enough to keep the old couple in comfort all their lives, and he himself lived in great state. He knighted the monkey, the dog and the pheasant, and made them his body-guard. Then he married a beautiful princess and lived happily till he died.

THE FOX AND THE BADGER.

THERE is a certain mountainous district in Shikoku in which a skillful hunter had trapped or shot so many foxes and badgers that only a few were left. These were an old grey badger and a female fox with one cub. Though hard pressed by hunger, neither dared to touch a loose piece of food, lest a trap might be hidden under it. Indeed they scarcely stirred out of their holes except at night, lest the hunter's arrow should strike them. At last the two animals held a council together to decide what to do, whether to emigrate or to attempt to outwit their enemy. They thought a long while, when finally the badger having hit upon a good plan, cried out:

"I have it. Do you transform yourself into a man. I'll pretend to be dead. Then you can bind me up and sell me in the town. With the money paid you can buy some food. Then I'll get loose and come back. The next week I'll sell you and you can escape."

"Ha! ha! ha! yoroshiu, yoroshiu," (good, good,) cried both together. "It's a capital plan," said Mrs. Fox.

So the Fox changed herself into a human form, and the badger, pretending to be dead, was tied up with straw ropes.

Slinging him over her shoulder, the fox went to town, sold the badger, and buying a lot of tofu (bean-cheese) and one or two chickens, made a feast. By this time the badger had got loose, for the man to whom he was sold, thinking him dead, had not watched him carefully. So scampering away to the mountains he met the fox, who congratulated him, while both feasted merrily.

The next week the badger took human form, and going to town sold the fox, who made believe to be dead. But the badger being an old skin-flint, and very greedy, wanted all the money and food for himself. So he whispered in the man's ear to watch the fox well as she was only feigning to be dead. So the man taking up a club gave the fox a blow on the head, which finished her. The badger, buying a good dinner, ate it all himself, and licked his chops, never even thinking of the fox's cub.

The cub after waiting a long time for its mother to come back, suspected foul play, and resolved on revenge. So going to the badger he challenged him to a trial of skill in the art of transformation. The badger accepted right off, for he despised the cub and wished to be rid of him.

"Well what do you want to do first? said Sir Badger."

"I propose that you go and stand on the Big Bridge leading to the city," said the cub, "and wait for my appearance. I shall come in splendid garments, and with many followers in my train. If you recognize me, you win, and I lose. If you fail, I win."

So the badger went and waited behind a tree. Soon a daimio riding in a palanquin, with a splendid retinue of courtiers appeared, coming up the road. Thinking this was the fox-cub changed into a nobleman, although wondering at the skill of the young fox, the badger went up to the palanquin and told the person inside that he was recognized and had lost the game.

"What!" said the daimio's followers, who were real men, and surrounding the badger, they beat him to death.

The fox-cub, who was looking on from a hill near by, laughed in derision, and glad that treachery was punished, scampered away.

THE SEVEN PATRONS OF HAPPINESS.

EVERY child knows who the Shichi fuku Fin or seven Patrons of Happiness are. They have charge of Long Life, Riches, Daily Food, Contentment, Talents, Glory, and Love. Their images carved in ivory, wood, stone, or cast in bronze are found in every house or sold in the stores or are painted on shop signs or found in picture books. They are a jolly company and make a happy family. On New Year's eve a picture of the Treasure-ship (Takaré-buné) laden with shippō (the seven jewels) and all the good things of life which men most desire is hung up in houses. The ship is coming into port and the passengers are the seven happy fairies who will make gifts to the people. These seven jewels are the same as those which Momotaro brought back from the oni's island.

First there is Fukoruku Jin the patron of Long Life or Length of Days. He has an enormously high forehead rounded at the top which makes his head look like a sugar-loaf. It is bald and shiny. A few stray white hairs sometimes sprout up, and the barber to reach them has to prop a ladder against his head to climb up and apply his razor. This big head comes from thinking so much. His eyebrows are cotton-white, and a long snowy beard falls down over his breast.

Once in a while in a good humor he ties a handkerchief over his high slippery crown and allows little boys to climb up on top—that is if they are good and can write well.

When he wants to show how strong and lively he is even though so old, he lets Daikoku the fat fellow ride on top of his head, while he smokes his pipe and wades across a river. Daikoku has to hold on tightly or he will slip down and get a ducking.

Usually the old shiny head is a very solemn gentleman, and walks slowly along with his staff in one hand while with the other he strokes his long eyebrows. The tortoise and the crane are always with him, for these are his pets. Sometimes a stag with hair white with age, walks behind him. Every body likes Fukoruku Jin because every one wants to get his favor and live long; until, like a lobster, their backs are bent with age. At a wedding you will always see a picture of white-bearded and shiny-pated Fukoruku Jin.

Daikoku is a short chubby fellow with eyes half sunk in fat but twinkling with fun. He has a flat cap set on his head like the kind which babies wear, a loose sack over his shoulders, and big boots on his feet. His throne is two straw bags of rice, and his badge of office is a mallet or hammer, which makes people rich when he shakes it. The hammer is the symbol of labor, showing that people may expect to get rich only by hard work. One end of it is carved to represent the jewel of the ebbing and the flowing tides, because merchants get rich by commerce on the sea and must watch the tides. He is often seen holding the arithmetic frame on which you can count, do sums, subtract, multiply, or divide, by sliding balls up and down a row of sticks set in a frame, instead of writing figures. Beside him is a ledger and day-book. His favorite animal is the rat, which like some rich men's pets, eats or runs away with his wealth.

The great silver-white radish called daikon, two feet long and as big as a man's calf is always seen near him because it signifies flourishing prosperity.

He keeps his bag tightly shut, for money easily runs away when the purse is once opened. He never lets go his hammer, for it is only by constant care that any one can keep money after he gets it. Even when he frolics with Fukuroku Jin, and rides on his head, he keeps his hammer ready swinging at his belt. He has huge lop ears.

Once in a while, when he wishes to take exercise, and Fukuroku Jin wants to show how frisky he can be, even if he is old, they have a wrestling match together. Daikoku nearly always beats, because Fukuroku Jin is so tall that he has to bend down to grip Daikoku, who is fat and short, and thus he becomes top-heavy. Then Daikoku gets his rival's long head under his left arm, seizes him over his back by the belt, and throws him over his shoulder flat on the ground. But if Fukuroku Jin can only get hold of Daikoku's lop ears, both fall together. Then they laugh heartily and try it again.

Ebisu is the patron of daily food, which is rice and fish, and in old times was chiefly fish. He is nearly as fat as Daikoku, but wears a court noble's high cap. He is always fishing or enjoying his game. When very happy, he sits on a rock by the sea, with his right leg bent under him, and a big red fish, called the tai, under his left arm. He carries a straw wallet on his back to hold his fish and keep it fresh. Often he is seen standing knee-deep in the water, pole in hand, watching for a nibble. Some say that Ebisu is the same scamp that goes by the other name of Sosanoō.

Hotei is the patron of contentment, and of course is the father of happiness. He does not wear much clothing, for the truth is that all his property consists of an old, ragged wrapper, a fan, and a wallet. He is as round as a pudding, and as fat as if rolled out of dough. His body is like a lump of mochi pastry, and his limbs like dango dumplings. He has lop ears that hang down over his shoulders, a tremendous double chin, and a round belly. Though he will not let his beard grow long, the slovenly old fellow never has it shaven when he ought to. He is a jolly vagabond, and never fit for company; but he is a great friend of the children, who romp over his knees and shoulders, pull his ears and climb up over his shaven head. He always keeps something good for them in his wallet. Sometimes he opens it wide, and then makes them guess what is inside. They try to peep in but are not tall enough to look over the edge. He makes tops, paints pictures or kites for the boys, and is the children's greatest friend. When the seven patrons meet together, Hotei is apt to drink more wine than is good for him.

Toshitoku is almost the only one of the seven who never lays aside his dignity. He has a very grave countenance. He is the patron of talents. His pet animal is a spotted fawn. He travels about a good deal to find and reward good boys, who are diligent in their studies, and men who are fitted to rule. In one hand he carries a crooked staff of bamboo, at the top of which is hung a book or roll of manuscript. His dress is like that of a learned doctor, with square cap, stole, and high-toed slippers.

Bishamon is the patron of glory and fame. He is a mighty soldier, with a golden helmet, breastplate and complete armor. He is the protector of priests and warriors. He gives them skill in fencing, horsemanship and archery. He holds a pagoda in one hand and a dragon sword in the other. His pet animal is the tiger.

Six out of the jolly seven worthies are men. Benten is the only lady. She is the patron of the family and of the sea. She plays the flute and the guitar for the others, and amuses them at their feasts, sometimes even dancing for them. Her real home is in Riu Gu, and she is the Queen of the world under the sea. She often dwells in the sea or ocean caves. Her favorite animal is the snake, and her servants are the dragons.

 Once a year the jolly seven meet together to talk over old times, relate their adventures, and have a supper together. Then they proceed to business, which is to arrange all the marriages for the coming year. They have a great many hanks of red and white silk, which are the threads of fate of those to be married: The white threads are the men, the red are the women. At first they select the threads very carefully, and tie a great many pairs or couples neatly and strongly together, so that the matches are perfect. All such marriages of threads make happy marriages among human beings. But by-and-by they get tired, and lazy, and instead of tying the knots carefully, they hurry up the work and then jumble them carelessly, and finally toss and tangle up all the rest in a muss.

 This is the reason why so many marriages are unhappy.

 Then they begin to frolic like big boys. Benten plays the guitar, and Bishamon lies down on the floor resting with his elbows to hear it. Hotei drinks wine out of a shallow red cup as wide as a dinner plate. Daikoku and Fukuroku Jin begin to wrestle, and when Daikoku gets his man down, he pounds his big head with an empty gourd while Toshitoku and Ebisu begin to eat tai fish. When this fun is over, Benten and Fukuroku Jin play a game of checkers, while the others look on and bet; except Hotei the fat fellow, who is asleep. Then they get ashamed of themselves for gambling, and after a few days the party breaks up and each one goes to his regular business again.

DAIKOKU AND THE ONI.

A

A LONG WHILE AGO, when the idols of Buddha and his host of disciples came to Japan, after traveling through China from India, they were very much vexed because the people still liked the little black fellow named Daikoku. Even when they became Buddhists they still burned incense to Daikoku, because he was the patron of wealth; for everybody then, as now, wanted to be rich. So the Buddhist idols determined to get rid of the little fat fellow. How to do it was the question. At last they called Yemma, the judge of the lower regions, and gave him the power to destroy Daikoku.

Now Yemma had under him a whole legion of oni, some green, some black, others blue as indigo, and others of a vermillion color, which he usually sent on ordinary errands.

But for so important an expedition he now called Shino a very cunning old fellow, and ordered him to kill or remove Daikoku out of the way.

Shino made his bow to his master, tightened his tiger-skin belt around his loins and set off.

It was not an easy thing to find Daikoku, even though every one worshipped him. So the oni had to travel a long way, and ask a great many questions of people, and often lose his way before he got any clue. One day he met a sparrow who directed him to Daikoku's palace, where among all his money-bags and treasure piled to the ceiling, the fat and lop-eared fellow was accustomed to sit eating daikon radish, and amuse himself with his favorite pets, the rats. Around him was stored in straw bags his rice which he considered more precious than money.

Entering the gate, the oni peeped about cautiously but saw no one. He went further on till he came to a large store house standing alone and built in the shape of a huge rice-measure. Not a door or window could be seen, but climbing up a narrow plank set against the top edge he peeped over, and there sat Daikoku.

The oni descended and got into the room. Then he thought it would be an easy thing to pounce upon Daikoku. He was already chuckling to himself over the prospect of such wealth being his own, when Daikoku squeaked out to his chief rat.

"Nedzumi san, (Mr. Rat) I feel some strange creature must be near. Go chase him off the premises."

Away scampered the rat to the garden and plucked a sprig of holly with leaves full of thorns like needles. With this in his fore-paw, he ran at the oni, whacked him soundly, and stuck him all over with the sharp prickles.

The oni yelling with pain ran away as fast as he could run. He was so frightened that he never stopped until he reached Yemma's palace, when he fell down breathless. He then told his master the tale of his adventure, but begged that he might never again be sent against Daikoku.

So the Buddhist idols finding they could not banish or kill Daikoku, agreed to recognize him, and so they made peace with him and to this day Buddhists and Shintōists alike worship the fat little god of wealth.

When people heard how the chief oni had been driven away by only a rat armed with holly, they thought it a good thing to keep off all oni. So ever afterward, even to this day, after driving out all the bad creatures with parched beans, they place sprigs of holly at their door-posts on New Year's eve, to keep away the oni and all evil spirits.

BENKEI AND THE BELL.

ON ONE of the hills overlooking the blue sky's mirror of Lake Biwa, stands the ancient monastery of Miidera which was founded over 1,200 years ago, by the pious mikado Tenchi.

Near the entrance, on a platform constructed of stoutest timbers, stands a bronze bell five and a half feet high. It has on it none of the superscriptions so commonly found on Japanese bells, and though its surface is covered with scratches it was once as brilliant as a mirror. This old bell, which is visited by thousands of people from all parts of Japan who come to wonder at it, is remarkable for many things.

Over two thousand years ago, say the bonzes, it hung in the temple of Gihon Shoja in India which Buddha built. After his death it got into the possession of the Dragon King of the World under the Sea. When the hero Toda the Archer shot the enemy of the queen of the Under-world, she presented him with many treasures and among them this great bell, which she caused to be landed on the shores of the lake. Toda however was not able to remove it, so he presented it to the monks at Miidera. With great labor it was brought to the hill-top and hung in this belfry where it rung out daily matins and orisons, filling the lake and hill sides with sweet melody.

Now it was one of the rules of the Buddhists that no woman should be allowed to ascend the hill or enter the monastery of Miidera. The bonzes associated females and wicked influences together. Hence the prohibition.

A noted beauty of Kioto hearing of the polished face of the bell, resolved in spite of the law against her sex to ascend the hill to dress her hair and powder her face in the mirror-like surface of the bell.

So selecting an hour when she knew the priests would be too busy at study of the sacred rolls to notice her, she ascended the hill and entered the belfry. Looking into the smooth surface, she saw her own sparkling eyes, her cheeks, flushed rosy with exercise, her dimples playing, and then her whole form reflected as in her own silver mirror, before which she daily sat. Charmed as much by the vastness as the brilliancy of the reflection, she stretched forth her hand, and touching her finger-tips to the bell prayed aloud that she might possess just such a mirror of equal size and brightness.

But the bell was outraged at the impiety of the woman's touch, and the cold metal shrank back, leaving a hollow place, and spoiling the even surface of the bell. From that time forth the bell gradually lost its polish, and became dull and finally dark like other bells.

When Benkei was a monk, he was possessed of a mighty desire to steal this bell and hang it up at Hiyeisan. So one night he went over to Miidera hill and cautiously crept up to the belfry and unhooked it from the great iron link which held it. How to get it down the mountain was now the question.

Should he let it roll down, the monks at Miidera would hear it bumping over the stones. Nor could he carry it in his arms, for it was too big around (16 feet) for him to grasp and hold. He could not put his head in it like a candle in a snuffer, for then he would not be able to see his way down.

So climbing into the belfry he pulled out the cross-beam with the iron link, and hanging on the bell put the beam on his shoulder to carry it in tembimbo style, that is, like a pair of scales.

The next difficulty was to balance it, for he had nothing but his lantern to hang on the other end of the beam to balance the bell. It was a prodigiously hard task to carry his burden the six or seven miles distance to Hiyeisan. It was "trying to balance a bronze bell with a paper lantern."

The work made him puff and blow and sweat until he was as hungry as a badger, but he finally succeeded in hooking it up in the belfry at Hiyeisan.

Then all the fellow priests of Benkei got up, though at night, to welcome him. They admired his bravery and strength and wished to strike the bell at once to show their joy.

"No, I won't lift a hammer or sound a note till you make me some soup. I am terribly hungry," said Benkei, as he sat down on a cross piece of the belfry and wiped his forehead with his cowl.

Then the priests got out the iron soup-pot, five feet in diameter, and kindling a fire made a huge mess of soup and served it to Benkei. The lusty monk sipped bowl after bowl of the steaming nourishment until the pot was empty.

"Now," said he, "you may sound the bell."

Five or six of the young bonzes mounted the platform and seized the rope that held the heavy log suspended from the roof. The manner of striking the bell was to pull back the log several feet, then let go the rope, holding the log after the rebound.

At the first stroke the bell quivered and rolled out a most mournful and solemn sound which as it softened and died away changed into the distinct murmur:

"I want to go back to Miidera, I want to go back to Miidera, I want to go-o back to-o M-i-i-de-ra-ra-a-a-a."

"Naru hodo" said the priests. "What a strange bell. It wants to go back. It is not satisfied with our ringing."

"Ah! I know what is the matter" said the aged abbot. "It must be sprinkled with holy water of Hiyeisan. Then it will be happy with us. Ho! page bring hither the deep sea shell full of sacred water."

So the pure white shell full of the consecrated water was brought, together with the holy man's brush. Dipping it in the water the abbot sprinkled the bell inside and out.

"I dedicate thee, oh bell, to Hiyeisan. Now strike," said he, signalling to the bell-pullers.

Again the young men mounted the platform, drew back the log with a lusty pull and let fly.

"M-m-m-mi-mi-de-de-ra-ra ye-e-e-e-ko-o-o-o-o" "(Miidera ye ko, I want to go back to Miidera)" moaned out the homesick bell.

This so enraged Benkei that he rushed to the rope waved the monks aside and seizing the rope strained every muscle to jerk the beam its entire length afield, and then let fly with force enough to crack the bell. For a moment the dense volume of sound filled the ears of all like a storm, but as the vibrations died away, the bell whined out:

"Miidera-mi-mi-de-de-ra-a-a ye-e-e-ko-o-o-o-o." "I want to go back to Miidera," sobbed the bell.

Whether struck at morning, noon or night the bell said the same words. No matter when, by whom, how hard or how gently it was struck, the bell moaned the one plaint as if crying, "I want to go back to Miidera." "I want to go back to Miidera."

At last Benkei in a rage unhooked the bell, shouldered it beam and all, and set off to take it back. Carrying the bell to the top of Hiyeisan, he set it down, and giving it a kick rolled it down the valley toward Miidera, and left it there. Then the Miidera bonzes hung it up again. Since that time the bell has completely changed its note, until now it is just like other bells in sound and behavior.

LITTLE SILVER'S DREAM OF THE SHOJI.

K

KO GIN SAN (Miss Little Silver) was a young maid who did not care for strange stories of animals, so much as for those of wonder-creatures in the form of human beings. Even of these, however, she did not like to dream, and when the foolish old nurse would tell her ghost stories at night, she was terribly afraid they would appear to her in her sleep.

To avoid this, the old nurse told her to draw pictures of a tapir, on the sheet of white paper, which, wrapped round the tiny pillow, makes the pillow-case of every young lady, who rests her head on two inches of a bolster in order to keep her well-dressed hair from being mussed or rumpled.

Old grannies and country folks believe that if you have a picture of a tapir under the bed or on the paper pillow-case, you will not have unpleasant dreams, as the tapir is said to eat them.

So strongly do some people believe this that they sleep under quilts figured with the device of this long-snouted beast. If in spite of this precaution one should have a bad dream, he must cry out on awaking, "tapir, come eat, tapir, come eat"; when the tapir will swallow the dream, and no evil results will happen to the dreamer.

Little Silver listened with both eyes and open mouth to this account of the tapir, and then making the picture and wrapping it around her pillow, she fell asleep. I suspect that the kowameshi (red rice) of which she had eaten so heartily at supper time, until her waist strings tightened, had something to do with her travels in dream-land.

She thought she had gone down to Ozaka, and there got on a junk and sailed far away to the southwest, through the Inland sea. One night the water seemed full of white ghosts of men and women. Some of them were walking on, and in, the water. Some were running about. Here and there groups appeared to be talking together. Once in a while the junk would run against one of them; and when Little Silver looked to see if he were hurt or knocked over, she could see nothing until the junk passed by, when the ghost would appear standing in the same place, as though the ship had gone through empty air.

Occasionally a ghost would come up to the side of the ship, and in a squeaky voice ask for a dipper. While she would be wondering what a ghost wanted to do with a dipper, a sailor would quietly open a locker, take out a dipper having no bottom, and give one every time he was asked for them. Little Silver noticed a large bundle of these dippers ready. The ghosts would then begin to bail up water out of the sea to empty it in the boat. All night they followed the junk, holding on with one hand to the gunwale, while they vainly dipped up water with the other, trying to swamp the boat. If dippers with bottoms in them had been given them, the sailors said, the boat would have been sunk. When daylight appeared the shadowy host of people vanished.

In the morning they passed an island, the shores of which were high rocks of red coral. A great earthen jar stood on the beach, and around it lay long-handled ladles holding a half-gallon or more, and piles of very large shallow red lacquered wine cups, which seemed as big as the full moon. After the sun had been risen some time, there came down from over the hills a troop of the most curious looking people. Many were short, little wizen-faced folks, that looked very old; or rather, they seemed old before they ought to be. Some were very aged and crooked, with hickory-nut faces, and hair of a reddish gray tint. All the others had long scarlet locks hanging loose over their heads, and streaming down their backs. Their faces were flushed as if by hard drinking, and their pimpled noses resembled huge red barnacles. No sooner did they arrive at the great earthen jar than they ranged themselves round it. The old ones dipped out ladles full, and drank of the wine till they reeled. The younger ones poured the liquor into cups and drank. Even the little infants guzzled quantities of the yellow saké from the shallow cups of very thin red-lacquered wood.

Then began the dance, and wild and furious it was. The leather-faced old sots tossed their long reddish-grey locks in the air, and pirouetted round the big saké jar. The younger ones of all ages clapped their hands, knotted their handkerchiefs over their foreheads, waved their dippers or cups or fans, and practiced all kinds of antics, while their scarlet hair streamed in the wind or was blown in their eyes.

The dance over, they threw down their cups and dippers, rested a few minutes and then took another heavy drink all around.

"Now to work" shouted an old fellow whose face was redder than his half-bleached hair, and who having only two teeth like tusks left looked just like an oni (imp.) As for his wife, her teeth had long ago fallen out and the skin of her face seemed to have added a pucker for every year since a half century had rolled over her head.

Then Little Silver looked and saw them scatter. Some gathered shells and burned them to make lime. Others carried water and made mortar, which they thickened by a pulp made of paper, and a glue made by boiling fish skin. Some dived under the sea for red coral, which they hauled up by means of straw ropes, in great sprigs as thick as the branches of a tree. They quickly ran up a scaffold, and while some of the scarlet-headed plasterers smeared the walls, others below passed up the tempered mortar on long shell shovels, to the hand mortar-boards. Even at work they had casks and cups of saké at hand, while children played in the empty kegs and licked the gummy sugar left in some of them.

"What is that house for?" asked Little Silver of the sailors.

"Oh, that is the Kura (storehouse) in which the King of the Shōji stores the treasures of life, and health, and happiness, and property, which men throw away, or exchange for the saké, which he gives them, by making funnels of themselves."

"Oh, Yes," said Little Silver to herself, as she remembered how her father had said of a certain neighbor who had lately been drinking hard, "he swills saké like a Shōji."

She also understood why picnic or "chow-chow" boxes were often decorated with pictures of Shōji, with their cups and dippers. For, at these picnics, many men get drunk; so much so indeed, that after a while the master of the feast orders very poor and cheap wine to be served to the guests. He also replaces the delicate wine cups of egg-shell porcelain, with big thick tea-cups or wooden bowls, for the guests when drunk, do not know the difference.

She also now understood why it was commonly said of a Mr. Matsu, who had once been very rich but was now a poor sot, "His property has all gone to the Shōji."

Just then the ship in which she was sailing struck a rock, and the sudden jerk woke up Little Silver, who cried out, "Tapir, come eat; tapir, come eat."

No tapir came, but if he had I fear Little Silver would have been more frightened than she was by her dream of the ghosts; for next morning she laughed to think how they had all their work a-dipping water for nothing, and at her old nurse for thinking a picture of a tapir could keep off dreams.

THE TENGUS, OR THE ELVES WITH LONG NOSES.

(After Hokusai.)

CURIOUS CREATURES are the tengus, with the head of a hawk and the body of a man. They have very hairy hands or paws with two fingers, and feet with two toes. They are hatched out of eggs, and have wings and feathers, until full grown. Then their wings moult, and the stumps are concealed behind their dress, which is like that of a man. They walk, when grown up, on clogs a foot high, which are like stilts, as they have but one support instead of two, like the sort which men wear. The tengus strut about easily on these, without stumbling.

The Dai Tengu, or master, is a solemn-faced, scowling individual with a very proud expression, and a nose about eight finger-breadths long. When he goes abroad, his retainers march before him, for fear he might break his nose against something. He wears a long grey beard down to his girdle, and moustaches to his chin. In his left hand he carries a large fan made of seven wide feathers. This is the sign of his rank. He has a mouth, but he rarely opens it. He is very wise, and rules over all the tengus in Japan.

The Karasu or crow-tengu is a black fellow, with a long beak, in the place where his nose and mouth ought to be. He looks as if some one had squeezed out the lower part of his face, and pulled his nose down so as to make a beak like a crow's. He is the Dai Tengu's lictor. He carries the axe of authority over his left shoulder, to chop bad people's heads off. In his right fist is his master's book of wisdom, and roll of authority. Even these two highest in authority in Tengu-land are servants of the great lord Kampira, the long-haired patron of sailors and mountaineers.

The greatest of the Dai Tengu lived in Kurama mountain and taught Yoshitsuné. This lad, while a pupil in the monastery, would slip out in the evening, when the priests thought him asleep, and come to the King of the Tengus, who instructed him in the military arts, in cunning, magic, and wisdom. Every night the boy would spread the roll of wisdom before him, and sit at the feet of the hoary-headed tengu, and learn the strange letters in which tengu wisdom is written, while the long-nosed servant tengus, propped up on their stilt-clogs, looked on. The boy was not afraid, but quickly learned the knowledge which birds, beasts and fishes have, how to understand their language and to fly, swim and leap like them.

When a tengu stumbles and falls down on his nose, it takes a long while to heal, and if he breaks it, the doctor puts it in splints like a broken arm, until it straightens out and heals up again.

Some of the amusements in Tengu-land are very curious. A pair of young tengus will fence with their noses as if they were foils. Their faces are well protected by masks, for if one tengu should "poke his nose" into the other's eye he might put it out, and a blind tengu could not walk about, because he would be knocking his nose against everything.

Two old tengus with noses nearly two feet long, sometimes try the strength of their face-handles. One fellow has his beak straight up in the air like a supporting post, while the other sits a yard off with his elastic nose stretched across like a tight-rope, and tied with twine at the top of the other one's nose. On this tight nose-rope a little tengu boy, with a tiny pug only two inches long, dances a jig. He holds an umbrella in his hand, now dancing, and now standing upon one foot. The tengu-daddy, whose nose serves as a tent-pole, waves his fan and sings a song, keeping time to the dance.

There is another tengu who sometimes quarrels with his wife, and when angry boxes her ears with his nose.

A lady-tengu who is inclined to be literary and sentimental, writes poetry. When the mood seizes her she ties the pen to her nose, dips it in ink and writes a poem on the wall.

A tengu-painter makes a long-handled brush to whitewash the ceiling, by strapping it to his nose.

Sometimes the little tengus get fighting, and then the feathers fly as they tear each other with their little claws which have talons on them shaped like a chicken's, but which when fully grown look like hands.

All the big tengus are fond of trying the strength of their noses, and how far they can bend them up and down without breaking. They have two favorite games of which they sometimes give exhibitions. The player has long strings of iron cash (that is, one hundred of the little iron coins, with a square hole in the centre). Several of these he slides on a rope like buttons on a string, or counters on a wire. Then he lifts them off with the tip of his nose. Sometimes his nose bends so much under the weight that the coins slip off. Whichever tengu can pick off the greater number of strings without letting any slip, wins the game, and is called O-hana (The King of Noses).

Another balances hoops and poles on his nose and throws balls through the hoops; or he poises a saucer of water on the tip of his nose without spilling a drop. Another fellow hangs a bell from the ceiling. Then, with a handkerchief tied loosely round his head, he pulls his nose back like a snapping-turtle's beak, and then suddenly lets go. His nose then strikes the bell and rings it. It hurts very much, but he does not mind it.

The tengus have one great fault. They love liquor too much. They often get drunk. They buy great casks of rice-wine, sling them round their necks, and drink out of long cups shaped like their faces, using the nose for a handle. A drunken tengu makes a funny sight, as he staggers about with his big wings drooping and flapping around him, and the feathers trailing in the mud, and his long nose limp, pendulous and groggy.

When the master of the tengus wishes to "see the flowers," which means to go on a picnic, he punishes his drunken servant by swinging the box of eatables over the fellow's red nose. Putting the end over his shoulders, he compels the sot to come along. It sobers the fellow, for the weight on his nose and the pulling on it hurts dreadfully, and often makes him squeal.

Oyama, a mountain near Tokio, is said to be full of these long-nosed elves, but many other mountains are inhabited by them, for they like lonely places away from men.

Dancers often put on masks like the tengu's face and dance a curious dance which they call the Tengu's quadrille.

The tengus are very proud fellows, and think themselves above human beings. They are afraid of brave men, however, and never dare to hurt them. They scare children, especially bad boys.

They watch a boy telling lies and catch him. Then the tengus pull out his tongue by the roots, and run away with it.

When a tengu walks, he folds his arms, throws back his head till his nose is far up in the air, and struts around as if he were a daimio. When a man becomes vain and carries his nose too high, the people say "He has become a tengu."

KINTARO, OR THE WILD BABY.

LONG, LONG AGO, when the tallest fir trees on the Hakoné mountains were no higher than a rice-stalk, there lived in that part of the range called Ashigara, a little ruddy boy, whom his mother had named Kintarō, or Golden Darling. He was not like other boys, for having no children to play with, he made companions of the wild animals of the forest.

He romped with the little bears, and often when the old she bear would come for her cubs to give them their supper and put them to bed, Kintarō would jump on her back and have a ride to her cave. He also put his arms around the neck of the deer, which were not afraid of him. He was prince of the forest, and the rabbits, wild boars, squirrels and martens, pheasants and hawks were his servants and messengers.

Although not much more than a fat baby, Kintarō wielded a big axe, and could chop a snake to pieces before he had time to wriggle.

Kintarō's father had been a brave soldier in Kiōto, who through the malice of enemies at court, had fallen into disgrace. He had loved a beautiful lady whom he married. When her husband died she fled eastward to the Ashigara mountains, and there in the lonely forests in which no human being except poor woodcutters ever came, her boy was born.

She lived in a cave, nourishing herself on roots and herbs. The woodcutters soon learned about the strange pair living wild but peacefully in the woods, though they did not dream of her noble rank. The boy was known among them as "Little Wonder," and the woman as "The old nurse of the mountain."

Thus, all alone, the little fellow grew up, exercising himself daily, so that even though a child he could easily wrestle with a bear. Among his retainers were the tengus, though they were often rebellious and disobedient, not liking to be governed by a boy.

One day, an old mother-tengu, who had always laughed at the idea of obeying a little dumpling of a fellow like Kintarō, flew up to her nest in a high fir tree. Kintarō watched to see where it was, and waited till she left it to go and seek for food. Then going up to the tree, he shook it with all his might, until the nest came tumbling down, and the two young squabs of tengus with it.

Now it happened that just at that time the great hero and imp-killer, Raikō, was marching through the mountains on his way to Kiōto. Seeing that the ruddy little fellow was no ordinary child, he found out the mother and heard her story. He then asked for the child and adopted him as his own.

So Kintarō went off with Raikō and grew up to be a brave soldier, and taking his father's name, he was known as Sakata Kintoki. His mother, however, remained in the mountains, and living to an extreme old age, was always known as "The old nurse of the mountains."

To this day, Kintaro is the hero of Japanese boys, and on their huge kites will usually be seen a picture of the little black-eyed ruddy boy of the mountains, with his axe, while around him are his wild playmates, and the young tengus rubbing their long noses, which were so nearly broken by their fall.

JIRAIYA, OR THE MAGIC FROG.

OGATA was the name of a castle-lord who lived in the Island of the Nine Provinces, (Kiushiu.) He had but one son, an infant, whom the people in admiration nicknamed Jiraiya (Young Thunder.) During one of the civil wars, this castle was taken, and Ogata was slain; but by the aid of a faithful retainer, who hid Jiraiya in his bosom, the boy escaped and fled northward to Echigo. There he lived until he grew up to manhood.

At that time Echigo was infested with robbers. One day the faithful retainer of Jiraiya being attacked, made resistance, and was slain by the robbers. Jiraiya now left alone in the world went out from Echigo and led a wandering life in several provinces.

All this time he was consumed with the desire to revive the name of his father, and restore the fortunes of his family. Being exceedingly brave, and an expert swordsman, he became chief of a band of robbers and plundered many wealthy merchants, and in a short time he was rich in men, arms and booty. He was accustomed to disguise himself, and go in person into the houses and presence of men of wealth, and thus learn all about their gates and guards, where they slept, and in what rooms their treasures were stored, so that success was easy.

Hearing of an old man who lived in Shinano, he started to rob him, and for this purpose put on the disguise of a pilgrim. Shinano is a very high table-land, full of mountains, and the snow lies deep in winter. A great snow storm coming on, Jiraiya took refuge in a humble house by the way. Entering, he found a very beautiful woman, who treated him with great kindness. This, however, did not change the robber's nature. At midnight, when all was still, he unsheathed his sword, and going noiselessly to her room, he found the lady absorbed in reading.

Lifting his sword, he was about to strike at her neck, when, in a flash, her body changed into that of a very old man, who seized the heavy steel blade and broke it in pieces as though it were a stick. Then he tossed the bits of steel away, and thus spoke to Jiraiya, who stood amazed but fearless:

"I am a man named Senso Dojin, and I have lived in these mountains many hundred years, though my true body is that of a huge frog. I can easily put you to death but I have another purpose. So I shall pardon you and teach you magic instead."

Then the youth bowed his head to the floor, poured out his thanks to the old man and begged to be received as his pupil.

Remaining with the old man of the mountain for several weeks, Jiraiya learned all the arts of the mountain spirits; how to cause a storm of wind and rain, to make a deluge, and to control the elements at will.

He also learned how to govern the frogs, and at his bidding they assumed gigantic size, so that on their backs he could stand up and cross rivers and carry enormous loads.

When the old man had finished instructing him he said "Henceforth cease from robbing, or in any way injuring the poor. Take from the wicked rich, and those who acquire money dishonestly, but help the needy and the suffering." Thus speaking, the old man turned into a huge frog and hopped away.

What this old mountain spirit bade him do, was just what Jiraiya wished to accomplish. He set out on his journey with a light heart. "I can now make the storm and the waters obey me, and all the frogs are at my command; but alas! the magic of the frog cannot control that of the serpent. I shall beware of his poison."

From that time forth the oppressed poor people rejoiced many a time as the avaricious merchants and extortionate money lenders lost their treasures. For when a poor farmer, whose crops failed, could not pay his rent or loan on the date promised, these hard-hearted money lenders would turn him out of his house, seize his beds and mats and rice-tub, and even the shrine and images on the god-shelf, to sell them at auction for a trifle, to their minions, who resold them at a high price for the money-lender, who thus got a double benefit. Whenever a miser was robbed, the people said, "The young thunder has struck," and then they were glad, knowing that it was Jiraiya, (Young Thunder.) In this manner his name soon grew to be the poor people's watchword in those troublous times.

Yet Jiraiya was always ready to help the innocent and honest, even if they were rich. One day a merchant named Fukutaro was sentenced to death, though he was really not guilty. Jiraiya hearing of it, went to the magistrate and said that he himself was the very man who committed the robbery. So the man's life was saved, and Jiraiya was hanged on a large oak tree. But during the night, his dead body changed into a bull-frog which hopped away out of sight, and off into the mountains of Shinano.

At this time, there was living in this province, a young and beautiful maiden named Tsunadé. Her character was very lovely. She was always obedient to her parents and kind to her friends. Her daily task was to go to the mountains and cut brushwood for fuel. One day while thus busy singing at the task, she met a very old man, with a long white beard sweeping his breast, who said to her:

"Do not fear me. I have lived in this mountain many hundred years, but my real body is that of a snail. I will teach you the powers of magic, so that you can walk on the sea, or cross a river however swift and deep, as though it were dry land."

Gladly the maiden took daily lessons of the old man, and soon was able to walk on the waters as on the mountain paths. One day the old man said, "I shall now leave you and resume my former shape. Use your power to destroy wicked robbers. Help those who defend the poor. I advise you to marry the celebrated man Jiraiya, and thus you will unite your powers."

Thus saying, the old man shrivelled up into a snail and crawled away.

"I am glad," said the maiden to herself, "for the magic of the snail can overcome that of the serpent. When Jiraiya, who has the magic of the frog, shall marry me, we can then destroy the son of the serpent, the robber named Dragon-coil (Orochimaru)."

By good fortune, Jiraiya met the maiden Tsunadé, and being charmed with her beauty, and knowing her power of magic, sent a messenger with presents to her parents, asking them to give him their daughter to wife. The parents agreed, and so the young and loving couple were married.

Hitherto when Jiraiya wished to cross a river he changed himself into a frog and swam across; or, he summoned a bull-frog before him, which increased in size until as large as an elephant. Then standing erect on his warty back, even though the wind blew his garments wildly, Jiraiya reached the opposite shore in safety. But now, with his wife's powers, the two, without any delay, walked over as though the surface was a hard floor.

Soon after their marriage, war broke out in Japan between the two famous clans of Tsukikagé and Inukagé. To help them fight their battles, and capture the castles of their enemies, the Tsukikagé family besought the aid of Jiraiya, who agreed to serve them and carried their banner in his back. Their enemies, the Inukagé, then secured the services of Dragon-coil.

This Orochimaru, or Dragon-coil, was a very wicked robber whose father was a man, and whose mother was a serpent that lived in the bottom of Lake Takura. He was perfectly skilled in the magic of the serpent, and by spurting venom on his enemies, could destroy the strongest warriors.

Collecting thousands of followers, he made great ravages in all parts of Japan, robbing and murdering good and bad, rich and poor alike. Loving war and destruction he joined his forces with the Inukagé family.

Now that the magic of the frog and snail was joined to the one army, and the magic of the serpent aided the other, the conflicts were bloody and terrible, and many men were slain on both sides.

On one occasion, after a hard fought battle, Jiraiya fled and took refuge in a monastery, with a few trusty vassals, to rest a short time. In this retreat a lovely princess named Tagoto was dwelling. She had fled from Orochimaru, who wished her for his bride. She hated to marry the offspring of a serpent, and hoped to escape him. She lived in fear of him continually. Orochimaru hearing at one time that both Jiraiya and the princess were at this place, changed himself into a serpent, and distilling a large mouthful of poisonous venom, crawled up to the ceiling in the room where Jiraiya and his wife were sleeping, and reaching a spot directly over them, poured the poisonous venom on the heads of his rivals. The fumes of the prison so stupefied Jiraiya's followers, and even the monks, that Orochimaru, instantly changing himself to a man, profited by the opportunity to seize the princess Tagoto, and make off with her.

Gradually the faithful retainers awoke from their stupor to find their master and his beloved wife delirious, and near the point of death, and the princess gone.

"What can we do to restore our dear master to life?" This was the question each one asked of the others, as with sorrowful faces and weeping eyes they gazed at the pallid forms of their unconscious master and his consort. They called in the venerable abbot of the monastery to see if he could suggest what could be done.

"Alas!" said the aged priest, "there is no medicine in Japan to cure your lord's disease, but in India there is an elixir which is a sure antidote. If we could get that, the master would recover."

"Alas! alas!" and a chorus of groans showed that all hope had fled, for the mountain in India, where the elixir was made, lay five thousand miles from Japan.

Just then a youth named Rikimatsu, one of the pages of Jiraiya, arose to speak. He was but fourteen years old, and served Jiraiya out of gratitude, for he had rescued his father from many dangers and saved his life. He begged permission to say a word to the abbot, who, seeing the lad's eager face, motioned to him with his fan to speak.

"How long can our lord live," asked the youth.

"He will be dead in thirty hours," answered the abbot, with a sigh.

"I'll go and procure the medicine, and if our master is still living when I come back, he will get well."

Now Rikimatsu had learned magic and sorcery from the Tengus, or long-nosed elves of the mountains, and could fly high in the air with incredible swiftness. Speaking a few words of incantation, he put on the wings of a Tengu, mounted a white cloud and rode on the east wind to India, bought the elixir of the mountain spirits, and returned to Japan in one day and a night.

On the first touch of the elixir on the sick man's face he drew a deep breath, perspiration glistened on his forehead, and in a few moments more he sat up.

Jiraiya and his wife both got well, and the war broke out again. In a great battle Dragon-coil was killed and the princess rescued. For his prowess and aid Jiraiya was made daimio of Idzu.

Being now weary of war and the hardships of active life, Jiraiya was glad to settle down to tranquil life in the castle and rear his family in peace. He spent the remainder of his days in reading the books of the sages, in composing verses, in admiring the flowers, the moon and the landscape, and occasionally going out hawking or fishing. There, amid his children and children's children, he finished his days in peace.

HOW THE JELLY-FISH LOST ITS SHELL.

PARTS of the seas of the Japanese Archipelago are speckled with thousands of round white jelly-fish, that swim a few feet below the surface. One can see the great steamer go ploughing through them as through a field of frosted cakes. The huge paddle-wheels make a perfect pudding of thousands of them, as they are dashed against the paddle-box and whipped into a froth like white of eggs or churned into a thick cream by the propeller blades. Sometimes the shoals are of great breadth, and then it veritably looks as though a crockery shop had been upset in the ocean, and ten thousand white dinner-plates had broken loose. Around the bays and harbors the Japanese boys at play drive them with paddles into shoals, and sometimes they poke sticks through them. This they can do easily, because the jelly-fish has no jacket of shell or bone like the lobster, nor any skin like a fish, and so always has to swim naked, exposed to all kinds of danger. Sometimes great jelly-fishes, two or three feet in diameter, sail gaily along near the shore, as proud as the long-handled-umbrella of a daimiō, and as brilliantly colored as a Japanese parasol. Floating all around their bodies, like the streamers of a temple festival, or a court lady's ribbons, are their long tentacles or feelers. No peacock stretching his bannered tail could make a finer sight, or look prouder than these floating sun-fishes, or bladders of living jelly.

But alas for all things made of water! Let but a wave of unusual force, or a sudden gust of wind come, and this lump of pride lies collapsed and stranded on the shore, like a pancake upset into a turnover, in which batter and crust are hopelessly mixed together. When found fresh, men often come down to the shore and cutting huge slices of blubber, as transparent as ice, they eat the solid water with their rice, in lieu of drink.

A jelly-fish as big as an umbrella, and weighing as much as a big boy, will, after lying a few hours in the sun leave scarcely a trace on the spot for their bodies are little more than animated masses of water. At night, however where a jelly-fish has stranded, the ground seems to crawl and emit a dull fire of phosphorescence which the Japanese call "dragon's light."

But the jelly-fish once had a shell, and was not so defenceless, say the fairy tales. How it lost it is thus told.

In the days of old, the jelly-fish was one of the retainers in waiting upon the Queen of the World under the Sea, at her palace in Riu Gu. In those days he had a shell, and as his head was hard, no one dared to insult him, or stick him with their horns, or pinch him with their claws, or scratch him with their nails, or brush rudely by him with their fins. In short, this fish instead of being a lump of jelly, as white and helpless as a pudding, as we see him now, was a lordly fellow that could get his back up and keep it high when he wished to. He waited on the queen and right proud was he of his office. He was on good terms with the King's dragon, which often allowed him to play with his scaly tail but never hurt him in the least.

One day the Queen fell sick, and every hour grew worse. The King became anxious, and her subjects talked about nothing else but her sickness. There was grief all through the water-world; from the mermaids on their beds of sponge, and the dragons in the rocky caverns, down to the tiny gudgeons in the rivers, that were considered no more than mere bait. The jolly cuttle-fish stopped playing his drums and guitar, folded his six arms and hid away moping in his hole. His servant the lobster in vain lighted his candle at night, and tried to induce him to come out of his lair. The dolphins and porpoises wept tears, but the clams, oysters and limpets shut up their shells and did not even wiggle. The flounders and skates lay flat on the ocean's floor, never even lifting up their noses. The squid wept a great deal of ink, and the jelly-fish nearly melted to pure water. The tortoise was patient and offered to do anything for the relief of the Queen.

But nothing could be done. The cuttle-fish who professed to be "a kind of a" doctor, offered the use of all his cups to suck out the poison, if that were the trouble.

But it wasn't. It was internal, and nothing but medicine that could be swallowed would reach the disease.

At last some one suggested that the liver of a monkey would be a specific for the royal sickness, and it was resolved to try it. The tortoise, who was the Queen's messenger, because he could live on both land and water, swim or crawl, was summoned. He was told to go upon earth to a certain mountain, catch a monkey and bring him alive to the Under-world.

Off started the tortoise on his journey to the earth, and going to a mountain where the monkeys lived, squatted down at the foot of a tree and pretended to be asleep though keeping his claws and tail out. There he waited patiently, well knowing that curiosity and the monkey's love of tricks would bring one within reach of his talons. Pretty soon, a family of chattering monkeys came running along among the branches overhead, when suddenly a young saru (monkey) caught sight of the sleeping tortoise.

"Naru hodo" (Is it possible?) said the long-handed fellow, "here's fun; let's tickle the old fellow's back and pull his tail."

All agreed, and forthwith a dozen monkeys, joining hand over hand, made a long ladder of themselves until they just reached the tortoise's back. (They didn't use their tails, for Japanese monkeys have none, except stumps two inches long). However, he who was to be the tail end of this living rope, when all was ready, crawled along and slipped over the whole line, whispering as he slid:

"'Sh! don't chatter or laugh, you'll wake the old fellow up."

Now the monkey expected to hold on the living pendulum by one long hand, and swinging down with the other, to pull the tortoise's tail, and see how near he could come to his snout without being snapped up. For a monkey well knew that a tortoise could neither jump off its legs nor climb a tree.

Once! Twice! The monkey pendulum swung back and forth without touching.

Three! Four! The monkey's finger-nails scratched the tortoise's back. Yet old Hard Shell pretended to be sound asleep.

Five! Six! The monkey caught hold of the tortoise's tail and jerked it hard. Old Tortoise now moved out its head a little, as if still only half awake.

Seven! Eight! This time the monkey intended to pull the tortoise's head, when just as he came within reach, the tortoise snapped him, held him in his claws, and as the monkey pendulum swung back he lost his hold. In an instant he was jerked loose, and fell head-foremost to the ground, half stunned.

Frightened at the loss of their end link, the other monkeys of the chain wound themselves up like a windlass over the branches, and squatting on the trees, set up a doleful chattering.

"Now," says the tortoise, "I want you to go with me. If you don't, I'll eat you up. Get on my back and I'll carry you; but I must hold your paw in my mouth so you won't run away."

Half frightened to death, the monkey obeyed, and the tortoise trotted off to the sea, swam to the spot over the Queen's palace, and in a fillip of the finger was down in the gardens of Riu Gu.

Here, let me say, that according to another version of this story the monkeys assembled in force when they suspected what the tortoise had come after, and catching him napping turned him over on his back so that he could not move or bite. Then they took his under shell off, so that he had to travel back to Riu Gu and get another one. This last version however is uncertain and it looks like a piece of invention

to suppose that the monkeys had a sufficient medical knowledge to make them suspicious of the design of the tortoise on the monkey's liver. I prefer the regular account.

THE MONKEYS IN GRIEF.

THE MONKEYS IN GRIEF.

The Queen hearing of the monkey's arrival thanked the tortoise, and commanded her cook and baker to feed him well and treat him kindly, for the queen felt really sorry because he was to lose his liver.

As for the monkey he enjoyed himself very much, and ran around everywhere amusing the star-fishes, clams, oysters and other pulpy creatures that could not run, by his rapid climbing of the rocks and coral bushes, and by rolling over the sponge beds and cutting all manner of antics.

They had never before seen anything like it. Poor fellow! he didn't suspect what was to come.

All this time however the jelly-fish pitied him in his heart, and could hardly keep what he knew to himself. Seeing that the monkey, lonely and homesick was standing by the shore of a pond, the jelly-fish squeezed himself up near him and said:

"Excuse my addressing you, I feel very sorry for you because you are to be put to death."

"Why?" said the monkey, "What have I done?"

"Oh, nothing," said the jelly-fish, "only our queen is sick and she wants your liver for medicine."

Then if ever any one saw a sick looking monkey it was this one. As the Japanese say "his liver was smashed." He felt dreadfully afraid. He put his hands over his eyes, and immediately began to plan how to save both his liver and his life.

After a while the rain began to fall heavily, and the monkey ran in out of the garden, and standing in the hall of the Queen's palace began to weep bitterly. Just then the tortoise, passing by, saw his captive.

"What are you crying about?"

"Aita! aita!" cried the monkey, "When I left my home on the earth, I forgot to bring my liver with me, but hung it upon a tree, and now it is raining and my liver will decay and I'll die. Aita!

aita!" and the poor monkey's eyes became red as a tai fish, and streamed with tears.

When the tortoise told the Queen's courtiers what the monkey had said, their faces fell.

"Why, here's a pretty piece of business. The monkey is of no use without his liver. We must send him after it."

So they dispatched the tortoise to the earth again, the monkey sitting a-straddle of his back. They came to the mountain again, and the tortoise being a little lazy, waited at the foot while the monkey scampered off, saying he would be back in an hour. The two creatures had become so well acquainted that the old Hard Shell fully trusted the lively little fellow.

But instead of an hour the tortoise waited till evening. No monkey came. So finding himself fooled, and knowing all the monkeys would take the alarm, he waddled back and told the Queen all about it.

"Then," said the Queen after reprimanding her messenger for his silly confidence, "the monkey must have got wind of our intention to use his liver, and what is more, some one of my retainers or servants must have told him."

Then the Queen issued an order commanding all her subjects to appear before the Dragon-King of the Sea. Whoever did this wicked thing, Kai Riu O would punish him.

Now it happened that all the fish and sea animals of all sorts, that swam, crawled, rolled or moved in any way, appeared before Kai Riu O, the Dragon-King, and his Queen—all except the jelly-fish. Then the Queen knew the jelly-fish was the guilty one. She ordered the culprit to be brought into her presence. Then publicly, before all her retainers and servants, she cried out:

"You leaky-tongued wretch, for your crime of betraying the confidence of your sovereign, you shall no longer remain among shell-fish. I condemn you to lose your shell."

Then she stripped off his shell, and left the poor jelly-fish entirely naked and ashamed.

"Be off, you tell-tale. Hereafter all your children shall be soft and defenceless."

The poor jelly-fish blushed crimson, squeezed himself out, and swam off out of sight. Since that time jelly-fishes have had no shells.

LORD CUTTLE-FISH GIVES A CONCERT.

DESPITE the loss of the monkey's liver, the queen of the World under the Sea, after careful attention and long rest, got well again, and was able to be about her duties and govern her kingdom well. The news of her recovery created the wildest joy all over the Under-world, and from tears and gloom and silence, the caves echoed with laughter, and the sponge-beds with music. Every one had on a "white face." Drums, flutes and banjos, which had been hung up on coral branches, or packed away in shell boxes, were taken down, or brought out, and right merrily were they struck or thrummed with the ivory hashi (plectrum). The pretty maids of the Queen put on their ivory thimble-nails, and the Queen again listened to the sweet melodies on the koto, (flat harp), while down among the smaller fry of fishy retainers and the scullions of the kitchen, were heard the constant thump of the tsutsumi (shoulder-drum), the bang of the taiko (big drum), and the loud cries of the dancers as they struck all sorts of attitudes with hands, feet and head.

No allusion was openly made either to monkeys, tortoises or jelly-fish. This would not have been polite. But the jelly-fish, in a distant pool in the garden, could hear the refrain, "The rivers of China run into the sea, and in it sinks the rain."

Now in the language of the Under-world people the words for "river," and "skin," (or "covering,") and "China," and "shell," and "rain," and "jelly," are the same. So the chorus, which was nothing but a string of puns, meant, "The skin of the jelly-fish runs to the sea, and in it sinks the jelly."

But none of these musical performances were worthy of the Queen's notice; although as evidences of the joy of her subjects, they did very well. A great many entertainments were gotten up to amuse the finny people, but the Queen was present at none of them except the one about to be described. How and why she became a spectator shall also be told.

One night the queen was sitting in the pink drawing-room, arrayed in her queenly robes, for she was quite recovered and expected to walk out in the evening. Everything in the room, except a vase of green and golden colored sponge-plant, and a plume of glass-thread, was of a pink color. Then there was a pretty rockery made of a pyramid of pumice, full of embossed rosettes of living sea-anemones of scarlet, orange, grey and black colors, which were trained to fold themselves up like an umbrella, or blossom out like chrysanthemums, at certain hours of the day, or when touched, behaving just like four o'clocks and sensitive plants.

All the furniture and hangings of the rooms were pink. The floor was made of mats woven from strips of shell-nacre, bound at the sides with an inch border of pink coral. The ceiling was made of the rarest of pink shells wrought into flowers and squares. The walls were decorated with the same material, representing sea-scenes, jewels and tortoise shell patterns. In the tokonoma, or raised space, was a bouquet of sea-weed of richest dyes, and in the nooks was an open cabinet holding several of the queen's own treasures, such as a tiara which looked like woven threads of crystal (Euplectella), and a toilet box and writing case made of solid pink coral.

The gem of all was a screen having eight folds, on which was depicted the palace and throne-room of Riu Gu, the visit of Toda, and the procession of the Queen, nobles and grandees that escorted the brave archer, when he took his farewell to return to earth.

The Queen sat on the glistening sill of the wide window looking out over her gardens, her two maids sitting at her feet. The sound of music wafted through the coral groves and crystal grottoes reached her ear.

"O medzurashi gozarimasu!" "(How wonderful this is!)" exclaimed the queen, half aloud. "What strange music is this? It is neither guitar, nor hand, nor shoulder drum, nor singing. It seems to be a mixture of all. Hear! It sounds as if a band with many instruments was playing to the accompaniment of a large choir of voices."

True enough! It was the most curious music ever heard in Riu Gu, for to tell the truth the voices were not in perfect accord, though all kept good time. The sound seemed to issue from the mansion of Lord Cuttle-fish, the palace physician. The queen's curiosity was roused.

"I shall go and see what it is," said she, as she rose up. Suddenly she recollected, and exclaimed:

"O, no, it would not be proper for me to be seen in public at this hour of the evening, and if it is in Lord Cuttle-fish's mansion, I could not enter without a retinue, No, it won't do for me, it's beneath my dignity," said her majesty to herself as she went over to touch her anemones, while her maids fanned her, seeing their mistress flushed with excitement, and fearing a relapse.

Curiosity got the better of the queenly lady, and off she started with only her two maids who held aloft over her head, the long pearl-handled fans made of white shark's fins.

"Besides," thought she, "perhaps the concert is outside, in the garden. If so, I can look down and see from the great green rock that overlooks it, and my lord Kai Riu O need not know of it."

The Queen walked over her pebbled garden walk, avoiding the great high road paved with white coral rock, and taking a by-path trimmed with fan-coral. The sound of the drums and voices grew louder, until as she reached the top of a green rock back of Lord Cuttle-fish's garden, the whole performance was open to her view.

It was so funny, and the queen was so overcome at the comical sight, that she nearly fell down and got the hysterics, laughing so heartily. She utterly forgot her dignity, and laughed till the tears ran down her face. She was so afraid she would scream out, that she nearly choked herself to death with her sleeve, while her alarmed maids, though meaning nothing by their acts but friendly help, slapped her back to give her breath.

There, at the top of a high green rock, all covered with barnacles, on a huge tuft of sponge, sat Lord Cuttle-fish, playing on three musical instruments at once. His great warty speckled head, six feet high, like a huge bag upside down, was bent forward to read the notes of his music book by the light of a wax candle, which was stuck in the feelers of a prickly lobster, and patiently held. Of his six pulpy arms one long one ran down like the trunk of an elephant, fingering along the pages of a music book. Two others were used to play the guitar, one to grasp the handle and pinch the strings, and the other to hold the ivory stick to strike the strings. The tsutsumi (small double drum) was held on his shoulder and neck, while still another arm curled up in a bunch, punched it like a fist. Below him was a another, a bass drum, set in a frame, and in his last leg, or arm, was clutched a heavy drum-stick, which pounded out tremendous noise, if not music. There the old fellow sat with his head bobbing, and all his six cuppy arms in motion, his rolling blue eyes ogling the notes, and his mouth like an elephant's, screeching out the song, which was made up of puns on 'tortoises,' 'monkeys,' 'jelly-fishes,' 'livers' and 'shell,' though the real words made an entirely different sense.

All this time, in front of Lord Cuttle-fish, sat the lobster holding up the light, like the kurombo, or black fellows who hold candles at the end of long-handled candle-sticks on the stage of the theatres so that the people may see the faces of the actors.

But the audience, or rather the orchestra was the funniest part of all. They could hardly be called listeners, for they were all performers. On the left was the lusty red-faced tai fish with its gills wide open, singing at the top, or rather at the bottom, of his throat, and beating time by flapping his wide fins. Just back of him was a little gudgeon, silent and fanning himself with a blue flat fan, having disgracefully broken down on a high note. Next behind, on the right, was a long-nosed gar-fish singing alto, and proud of her slender form, with the last new thing in folding fans held in her fin. In the fore-ground squatted a great fat frog with big bulging eyes, singing base, and leading the choir by flapping his webbed fingers up and down with his frightful cavern of a mouth wide open. Next, sat the stately and dignified mackerel who was rather scandalized at the whole affair, and kept very still, refusing to join in. At the mackerel's right fin, squeaked out the stupid flat-headed fugu fish with her big eye impolitely winking at the servant-maid just bringing in refreshments; for the truth was, she was thirsty after so much vocal exercise. The fugu was very vain and always played the coquette around the hooks of the fishermen who always liked to eat her because she was so sweet, yet her flesh was poison.

"How strange it is that men will angle after that ugly hussy, when she poisons them," was the oft-repeated remark of the gar-fish.

Just behind the herring, with one eye on Lord Cuttle-fish and one on the coming refreshments, was the skate. The truth must be told that the entire right wing of the orchestra was very much demoralized by the smell of the steaming tea and eatables just about to be served. The suppon, (tortoise with a snout like a bird's beak,) though he continued to sing, impolitely turned his head away from Lord Cuttle-fish, and his back to the frog that acted as precentor. The sucker, though very homely, and bloated with fat, kept on in the chorus, and pretended not to notice the waiter and her tray and cups. Indeed, Madame Sucker thought it quite vulgar in the tortoise to be so eager after the cakes and wine.

In truth the concert had been long, and all were thirsty and ready for a bite and a drink.

Suddenly the music ceased, and the long clatter on the drum announced the end. Lord Cuttle-fish kicked over his drum, unscrewed his guitar, and packed it away in his music box. He then slid along on his six slippery legs to the refreshments, and actually amused the company by standing on his head, and twirling his six cuppy arms around.

At this Miss Mackerel was quite shocked, and whispered under her fan to the gar-fish, "It is quite undignified. What would the Queen say if she saw it?" not knowing that the Queen was looking on.

Then all sat down on their tails, propped upright on one fin, and produced their fans to cool themselves off. The lobster pulled off the candle stump and ate it up, wiped his feelers, and joined the party.

The liquid refreshments consisted of sweet and clear saké (rice beer) tea, and cherry-blossom water. The solids were thunder-cakes, egg-cracknels, boiled rice, daikon radishes and macaroni, lotus-root, taro, and side-dishes piled up with flies, worms, bugs and all kinds of bait for the small fry—the finny brats that were to eat at the second table. The tea was poured by the servants of Lord Cuttle-fish. These were the funniest little green kappas, or creatures half way between a monkey and a tortoise, with yellow eyes, hands like an ape, hair clipped short on their heads, eyes like frogs, and a mouth that stretched from ear to ear Poor creatures! they were only too happy to know that though they looked like monkeys their livers would not do for medicine.

The Queen did not wait to see the end of the feast, but laughing heartily, returned to her palace and went to sleep.

After helping himself with all the cups of his arms out of the tub of boiled rice, until Miss Mackerel made up her mind that he was an omeshi gurai, (rice glutton,) and drinking like a shoal of fishes, Lord Cuttle-fish went home, coiled himself up into a ball, and fell asleep. He had a headache next morning.

YORIMASA, THE BRAVE ARCHER.

GENZAN YORIMASA was a brave warrior and a very useful man who lived more than eight thousand moons ago. On account of his valor and skill in the use of the bow he was called to Kioto, and promoted to be chief guard of the imperial palace. At that time the emperor, Narahito, could not sleep at night, because his rest was disturbed by a frightful beast, which scared away even the sentinels in armor who stood on guard.

This dreadful beast had the wings of a bird, the body and claws of a tiger, the head of a monkey, a serpent tail, and the crackling scales of a dragon. It came after night, upon the roof of the palace, and howled and scratched so dreadfully, that the poor mikado losing all rest, grew weak and thin. None of the guards dare face it in hand-to-hand fight, and none had skill enough to hit it with an arrow in the dark, though several of the imperial corps of archers had tried again and again. When Yorimasa received his appointment, he strung his bow carefully, and carefully honing his steel-headed arrows, stored his quiver, and resolved to mount guard that night with his favorite retainer.

It chanced to be a stormy night. The lightning was very vivid, and Kaminari, the thunder-god was beating all his drums. The wind swirled round frightfully, as though Fuden the wind-god was emptying all his bags. Toward midnight, the falcon eye of Yorimasa saw, during a flash of lightning, the awful beast sitting on the "devil's tile" at the tip of the ridge-pole, on the north-east end of the roof. He bade his retainer have a torch of straw and twigs ready to light at a moment's notice, to loosen his blade, and wet its hilt-pin, while he fitted the notch of his best arrow into the silk cord of his bow.

Keeping his eyes strained, he pretty soon saw the glare now of one eye, now two eyes, as the beast with swaying head crept along the great roof to the place on the eaves directly under the mikado's sleeping-room. There it stopped.

This was Yorimasa's opportunity. Aiming about a foot to the right of where he saw the eye glare, he drew his yard-length shaft clear back to his shoulder, and let fly. A dull thud, a frightful howl, a heavy bump on the ground, and the writhing of some creature among the pebbles, told in a few seconds time that the shaft had struck flesh. The next instant Yorimasa's retainer rushed out with blazing torch and joined battle with his dirk. Seizing the beast by the neck, he quickly despatched him, by cutting his throat. Then they flayed the monster, and the next morning the hide was shown to his majesty.

All congratulated Yorimasa on his valor and marksmanship. Many young men, sons of nobles and warriors, begged to become his pupils in archery. The mikado ordered a noble of very high rank to present to Yorimasa a famous sword named Shishi-no-ō, (King of Wild Boars), and to give him a lovely maid of honor named Ayami, to wife. And so the brave and the fair were married, and to this day the fame of Yorimasa is like the "umé-také-matsu," (plum-blossom, bamboo and pine), fragrant, green and ever-during.

YORIMASA AND THE NIGHT-BEAST.

YORIMASA AND THE NIGHT-BEAST.

WATANABE CUTS OFF THE ONI'S ARM.

W

WHEN the capital of Japan was the city of Kioto, and the mikado dwelt in it with all his court, there lived a brave captain of the guard named Yorimitsu, who belonged to the famous Minamoto family. He was also called Raiko, and by this name he is best known to all the boys and girls in Great Japan. Under Captain Raiko were three brave guardsmen, one of whom was named Watanabé Tsuna. The duty of these men-at-arms was to watch at the gates leading to the palace.

It had come to pass that the blossom capital had fallen in a dreadful condition, because the guards at the other gates had been neglected. Thieves were numerous and murders were frequent, so that every one in the city was afraid to go out into the streets at night. Worse than all else, was the report that oni or imps were prowling around in the dark to seize people by the hair of the head. Then they would drag them away to the mountains, tear the flesh off their bones, and eat them up.

The worst place in the city, to which the horned imps came oftenest, was at the south-western gate called the Rajo-mon.

To this post of danger, Raiko sent Tsuna, the bravest of his guards.

It was on a dark, rainy and dismal night, that Tsuna started, well-armed, to stand sentinel at the gate. His trusty helmet was knotted over his chin, and all the pieces of his armor were well laced up. His sandals were girt tight to his feet, and in his belt was thrust the trusty sword, freshly ground, until its edge was like a razor's, and with it the owner could cut asunder a hair floating in the air.

Arriving at the red pillar of the gate, Tsuna paced up and down the stone way with eyes and ears wide open. The wind was blowing frightfully, the storm howled and the rain fell in such torrents that soon the cords of Tsuna's armor and his dress were soaked through.

The great bronze bell of the temples on the hills boomed out the hours one after another, until a single stroke told Tsuna it was the hour of the Rat (midnight).

Two hours passed, and the hour of the Bull sounded (2 A.M.,) still Tsuna was wide awake. The storm had lulled, but it was darker than ever.

The hour of the Tiger (3 o'clock) rung out, and the soft mellow notes of the temple bell died away like a lullaby wooing one to sleep, spite of will and vow.

The warrior, almost without knowing it, grew sleepy and fell into a doze. He started and woke up. He shook himself, jingled his armor, pinched himself, and even pulled out his little knife from the wooden scabbard of his dirk, and pricked his leg with the point of it to keep awake, but all in vain. Unconsciously overcome, he leaned against the gate-post, and fell asleep.

This was just what the imp wanted. All the time he had been squatting on the cross-piece at the top of the gate waiting his opportunity. He now slid down as softly as a monkey, and with his iron-like claws grabbed Tsuna by the helmet, and began to drag him into the air.

In an instant Tsuna was awake. Seizing the hairy wrist of the imp with his left hand, with his right he drew his sword, swept it round his head, and cut off the demon's arm. The oni, frightened and howling with pain, leaped up the post and disappeared in the clouds.

Tsuna waited with drawn sword in hand, lest the oni might come again, but in a few hours morning dawned. The sun rose on the pagodas and gardens and temples of the capitol and the nine-fold circle of flowery hills. Everything was beautiful and bright. Tsuna returned to report to his captain, carrying the oni's arm in triumph. Raiko examined it, and loudly praised Tsuna for his bravery, and rewarded him with a silken sash.

Now it is said that if an oni's arm be cut off it cannot be made to unite with the body again, if kept apart for a week. So Raiko warned Tsuna to lock it up, and watch it night and day, lest it be stolen from him.

So Tsuna went to the stone-cutters who made idols of Buddha, mortars for pounding rice, and coffers for burying money in to be hidden away in the ground, and bought a strong box cut out of the solid stone. It had a heavy lid on it, which slid in a groove and came out only by touching a secret spring. Then setting it in his bed chamber, he guarded it day and night, keeping the gate and all his doors locked. He allowed no one who was a stranger to look at the trophy.

Six days passed by, and Tsuna began to think his prize was sure, for were not all his doors tight shut? So he set the box out in the middle of the room, and twisting some rice-straw fringe in token of sure victory and rejoicing, he sat down in ease before it. He took off his armor and put on his court robes. During the evening, but rather late, there was a feeble knock like that of an old woman at the gate outside.

Tsuna cried out, "Who's there?"

The squeaky voice of his aunt (as it seemed), who was a very old woman, replied "Me, I want to see my nephew, to praise him for his bravery in cutting the oni's arm off."

So Tsuna let her in and carefully locking the door behind her, helped the old crone into the room, where she sat down on the mats in front of the box and very close to it. Then she grew very talkative, and praised her nephew's exploit, until Tsuna felt very proud.

All the time the old woman's left shoulder was covered with her dress while her right hand was out. Then she begged earnestly to be allowed to see the limb. Tsuna at first politely refused, but she urged, until yielding affectionately he slid back the stone lid just a little.

"This is my arm" cried the old hag, turning into an oni, and dragging out the arm.

She flew up to the ceiling, and was out of the smoke-slide through the roof in a twinkling. Tsuna rushed out of the house to shoot her with an arrow, but he saw only a demon far off in the clouds grinning horribly. He noted carefully however that the direction of the imps' flight was to the north-west.

A council was now held by Raiko's band, and it was decided that the lurking-place of the demons must be in the mountains of Oyé in the province of Tango. It was resolved to hunt out and destroy the imps.

WATANABE KILLS THE GREAT SPIDER.

DURING the time in which Watanabé was forming his plan to destroy the onis that lurked in the Oyé mountains, the brave Raiko fell sick, and daily grew weaker and paler. When the demons found this out they sent the three-eyed imp called Mitsumé Kozo, to plague him.

This imp, which had a snout like a hog's, three monstrous blue eyes, and a mouth full of tusks, was glad that the brave soldier could no longer fight the onis. He would approach the sick man in his chamber, leer horribly at him, loll out his tongue, and pull down the lids of his eyes with his hairy fingers, until the sight sickened Raiko more and more.

But Raiko, well or ill, always slept with his trusty sword under his pillow, and pretending to be greatly afraid, and to cower under the bed-clothes, the kozo grew bolder and bolder. When the imp was near the bed, Raiko drew his blade, and cut the oni across his huge double nose. This made the demon howl, and he ran away, leaving tracks of blood.

When Tsuna and his band heard of their brave master's exploit, they came to congratulate him, and offered to hunt out the demon and destroy him.

They followed the red drops until they came to a cavern in the mountains. Entering this they saw in the gloom a spider six feet high, with legs as long as a fishing-pole, and as thick as a daikon radish. Two great yellow eyes glared at them like lamps. They noticed a great gaping wound as if done by a sword-cut on his snout.

It was a horrible, nasty hairy thing to fight with swords, since to get near enough, they would be in danger of the creature's claws. So Tsuna went and chopped down a tree as thick as a man's leg, leaving the roots on, while his comrades prepared a rope to tie up the monster like a fly in a web. Then with a loud yell Tsuna rushed at the spider, felled him with a blow, and held him down with the tree and roots so he could not bite or use his claws. Seeing this, his comrades rushed in, and bound the monster's legs tight to his body so that he could not move. Drawing their swords they passed them through his body and finished him. Returning in triumph to the city, they found their dear captain recovered from his illness.

Raiko thanked his brave warriors for their exploits, made a feast for them, and gave them many presents. At this feast Captain Raiko told them that he had received orders from the mikado to march against the oni's den in Tango, slaughter them all, and rescue the prisoners he should find there. Then he showed them his commission written in large letters,

"I command you, Raiko, to chastise the onis."

He also allowed them to examine the gold brocade bag, in which it was kept, and which one of the fair ladies of the court had made for him with her own tapering fingers.

At this time many families in Kioto were grieving over the loss of their children, and even while Tsuna had been away, several lovely damsels had been seized and taken to the demon's den.

Lest the onis might hear of their coming, and escape, the four trusty men disguised themselves as Komuso or wandering priests of the mountains. They put on over their helmets, huge hats like wash-bowls, made of straw, woven so tightly that no one could see their faces. They covered their armor with very cheap and common clothes, and then after worshipping at the shrines, began their march.

RAIKO AND THE SHI-TEN DOJI.

QUITE PATHLESS were the desolate mountains of Tango, for no one ever went into them except once in a while a poor woodcutter or charcoal-burner; yet Raiko and his men set out with stout hearts. There were no bridges over the streams, and frightful precipices abounded. Once they had to stop and build a bridge by felling a tree, and walking across it over a dangerous chasm. Once they came to a steep rock, to descend which they must make a ladder of creeping vines. At last they reached a dense grove at the top of a cliff, far up to the clouds, which seemed as if it might contain the demon's castle.

Approaching, they found a pretty maiden washing some clothes which had spots of blood on them. They said to her, "Sister, Miss, why are you here, and what are you doing?"

"Ah," said she, with a deep sigh, "you must not come here. This is the haunt of demons. They eat human flesh and they will eat yours." "Look there" said she pointing to a pile of white bones of men, women and children, "You must go down the mountain as quickly as you came." Saying this she burst into tears.

But instead of being frightened or sorrowful, the brave fellows nearly danced for joy. "We have come here for the purpose of destroying the demons by the mikado's orders," said Raiko, patting his breast, where inside his dress in the damask bag was the imperial order.

At this the maiden dried her tears and smiled so sweetly that Raiko's heart was touched by her beauty.

"But how came you to live among these cannibal demons," asked Raiko.

She blushed deeply as she replied sadly "Although they eat men and old women, they keep the young maidens to wait on them."

"It's a great pity" said Raiko, "but we shall now avenge our fellow subjects of the mikado, as well as your shame and cruel treatment, if you will show us the way up the cliff to the den."

They began to climb the hill but they had not gone far before they met a young oni who was a cook in the great dōji's kitchen. He was carrying a human limb for his master's lunch. They gnashed their teeth silently, and clutched their swords under their coats. Yet they courteously saluted the cook-demon, and asked for an interview with the chief. The demon smiled in his sleeve, thinking what a fine dinner his master would make of the four men.

A few feet forward, and a turn in the path brought them to the front of the demon's castle. Among tall and mighty boulders of rock, which loomed up to the clouds, there was an opening in the dense groves, thickly covered with vines and mosses like an arbor. From this point, the view over the plains below commanded a space of hundreds of miles. In the distance the red pagodas, white temple-gables and castle towers of Kioto were visible.

Inside the cave was a banqueting hall large enough to seat one hundred persons. The floor was neatly covered with new, clean mats of sea-green rice-straw, on which tables, silken cushions, arm-rests, drinking-cups, bottles and many other articles of comfort lay about. The stone walls were richly decorated with curtains and hangings of fine silken stuffs.

At the end of the long hall, on a raised dais, our heroes presently observed, as a curtain was lifted, the chief demon, Shi-ten dōji, of august, yet frightful appearance. He was seated on a heap of luxurious cushions made of blue and crimson crape, stuffed with swan's down. He was leaning on a golden arm-rest. His body was quite red, and he was round and fat like a baby grown up. He had very black hair cut like a small boy's, and on the top of his head, just peeping through the hair were two very short horns. Around him were a score of lovely maidens—the fairest of Kioto—on whose beautiful faces was stamped the misery they dared not fully show, yet could not entirely conceal. Along the wall other demons sat or lay at full length, each one with his handmaid seated beside him to wait on him and pour out his wine. All of them were of horrible aspect, which only made the beauty of the maidens more conspicuous. Seeing our heroes walk in the hall led by the cook, each one of the demons was as happy as a spider, when in his lurking hole he feels the jerk on his web-thread that tells him a fly is caught. All of them at once poured out a fresh saucer of saké and drank it down.

Raiko and his men separated, and began talking freely with the demons until the partitions at one corner were slid aside, and a troop of little demons who were waiter-boys entered. They brought in a host of dishes, and the onis fell to and ate. The noise of their jaws sounded like the pounding of a rice mill.

Our heroes were nearly sickened at the repast, for it consisted chiefly of human flesh, while the wine-cups were made of empty human skulls. However, they laughed and talked and excused themselves from eating, saying they had just lunched.

As the demons drank more and more they grew lively, laughed till the cave echoed, and sang uproarious songs. Every time they grinned, they showed their terrible tusks, and teeth like fangs. All of them had horns, though most of these were very short.

The dōji became especially hilarious, and drank the health of every one of his four guests in a skull full of wine. To supply him there was a tub full of saké at hand, and his usual drinking-vessel was a dish which seemed to Tsuma to be as large as a full moon.

Raiko now offered to return the courtesies shown them by dancing "the Kioto dance," for which he was famous. Stepping out into the centre of the hall, with his fan in one hand, he danced gracefully and with such wonderful ease, that the onis screamed with delight, and clapped their hands in applause, saying they had never seen anything to equal it. Even the maidens, lost in admiration of the polished courtier, forgot their sorrow, and felt as happy for the time as though they were at home dancing.

The dance finished, Raiko took from his bosom a bottle of saké, and offered it to the chief demon as a gift, saying it was the best wine of Sakai. The delighted dōji drank and gave a sip to each of his lords saying, "This is the best liquor I ever tasted, you must drink the health of our friends in it."

Now Raiko had bought, at the most skillful druggists' in the capital, a powerful sleeping potion, and mixed it with the wine, which made it taste very sweet. In a few minutes all the demons had dropped off asleep, and their snores sounded like the rolling thunder of the mountains.

Then Raiko rose up and gave the signal to his comrades. Whispering to the maidens to leave the room quietly, they drew their swords, and with as little noise as possible cut the throats of the demons. No sound was heard but the gurgling of blood that ran out in floods on the floor. The dōji lying like a lion on his cushions was still sleeping, the snores issuing out of his nose like thunder from a cloud. The four warriors approached him and like loyal vassals as they were, they first turned their faces towards Kioto, reverenced the mikado, and prayed for the blessing of the gods who made Japan. Raiko then drew near, and measuring the width of the doji's neck with his sword found that it would be short. Suddenly, the blade lengthened of itself. Then lifting his weapon, he smote with all his might and cut the neck clean through.

   In an instant, the bloody head flew up in the air gnashing its teeth and rolling its yellow eyes, while the horns sprouted out to a horrible length, the jaws opening and shutting like the edges of an earthquake fissure. It flew up and whirled round the room seven times. Then with a rush it flew at Raiko's head, and bit through the straw hat and into the iron helmet inside. But this final effort exhausted its strength, it's motions ceased and it fell heavily to the floor.

   Anxiously the comrades helped their fallen leader to rise, and examined his head. But he was unhurt,—not a scratch was on him. Then the heroes congratulated each other and after despatching the smaller demons, brought out all the treasure and divided it equally. Then they set the castle on fire and buried the bones of the victims, setting up a stone to mark the spot. All the maidens and captives were assembled together, and in great state and pomp they returned to Kioto. The virgins were restored to their parents, and many a desolate home was made joyful, and many mourning garments taken off. Raiko was honored by the mikado in being made a kugé (court noble,) and was appointed Chief of the entire garrison of Kiotō. Then all the people were grateful for his valor.

THE SAZAYE AND THE TAI.

SAZAYÉ is a shell-fish, which is very proud of its shell. This is high, full of points like towers, and thick like a castle wall. When feeding, enjoying itself or moving around, its long neck and body are stretched out before it, armed with its hard operculum, which is like an iron shield, or the end of a battering ram. The operculum fits the entrance to its shell like a trap door. As soon as any danger is near it pulls in its head, and slams itself shut with a loud noise.

On account of the hardness and thickness of his shell, the sazayé is the envy of the soft-bodied fishes that covet his security. But on the other hand the sazayé, though a slow moving creature, is apt to be too proud of his defence and trust too much to his fancied security.

One day a Tai (red fish) and a Herring were looking at the strong shell of the sazayé, and becoming quite envious, the Tai said:

"What a mighty strong castle you do live in, Mr. Sazayé. When you once shut up your shell no one need even try to touch you. You are to be envied sir."

The Sazayé was tickled at the flattery, but pretending to be very humble, shook his head and said:

"It is very kind in you, my lords, to say so, but my little hut is nothing but a shell; yet I must say that when I lock my door I do not feel any anxiety, and I really pity you poor fellows who have no shell at all."

He had hardly got the last word out of his grisly throat, when suddenly there was a great splash, and away darted the tai and herring, never resting their fins or tails a moment till safe out of danger.

The Sazayé drew in his flap in the twinkling of an eye, and keeping as quiet as possible, wondered what the noise was. Was it a stone, or a net, or a fish-hook? He wondered if the tai and herring were caught.

"Surely they must be," thought he. "However I'm safe, thanks to my castle shell," he muttered.

So drawing his trap tighter he took a long nap. When he woke up, quite refreshed, he cautiously loosened his trap and peeped out.

"How strange every thing looks, am I dreaming?" said he as he saw piles of fish, clams, prawns and lobsters lying on a board all around him.

"Ugh, what is that?" clapping himself shut as a great black-nosed and long-whiskered dog poked his muzzle near him.

Poor shell-fish! There he lay in a fishmonger's shop, with a slip of paper marked "ten cash," (1-10 of a cent,) on his back. A few hours later, purchased by a laborer's wife for his dinner, he was stewing along with several of his relative's in his own juice. The castle, of which he was so proud, serving first as a dinner-pot, then as a saucer, after which it was thrown away in a heap and burned into lime.

THE FISH STALL IN TOKIO.

THE FISH STALL IN TOKIO.

SMELLS AND JINGLES.

YEDO people are very fond of broiled eels. A rich merchant, named Kisaburo, who was very miserly with his money, once moved his quarters next door to the shop of one Kichibei, who caught and cooked eels for a living. During the night Mr. Kichibei caught his stock in trade, and in the day-time served them, smoking hot, to his customers. Cut into pieces three or four inches long, they were laid to sizzle on a grid-iron over red hot charcoal, which was kept in a glow by constant fanning.

Kisaburo, wishing to save money, and having a strong imagination, daily took his seat at meal time close to his neighbor's door. Eating his boiled rice, and snuffing in the odors of the broiled eels, as they were wafted in, he enjoyed with his nose, what he would not pay for to put in his mouth. In this way, as he flattered himself, he saved much money, and his strong box grew daily heavier.

Kichibei, the eel-broiler, on finding this out, thought he would charge his stingy neighbor for the smell of his eels. So, making out his bill he presented it to Kisaburo, who seemed to be much pleased. He called to his wife to bring his iron-bound money box, which was done. Emptying out the shining mass of kobans (oval gold pieces, worth five or six dollars), ichi-bu and ni-bu (square silver pieces, worth a quarter and a half dollar respectively) he jingled the coins at a great rate, and then touching the eel-man's bill with his fan, bowed, low and said with a smile:

A JINGLE FOR A SNIFF.

A JINGLE FOR A SNIFF.

"All right, neighbor Kichibei, we are square now."

"What!" cried the eel-frier, "are you not going to pay me?"

"Why yes, I have paid you. You have charged me for the smell of your eels, and I have paid you with the sound of my money."

THE LAKE OF THE LUTE AND THE MATCHLESS MOUNTAIN.

O OF ALL the beautiful objects in "the land of the holy gods," as the Japanese call their country, none are more beautiful than Fuji Mountain and Lake Biwa. The one is a great cone of white snow, the other is a sheet of heaven-blue water, in shape like a lute with four strings.

Sweeping from twenty square leagues of space out of the plain and rising twelve thousand feet in air, Fuji, or Fusi Yama, casts its sunset shadow far out on the ocean, and from fourteen provinces gleams the splendor of its snowy crest. It sits like a king on his throne in the heart of Suruga Province.

One hundred and thirty miles to the west as the crane wings her flight, in the heart of Omi, is Biwa Ko, the lake of the lute. It is sixty miles long and as blue as the sky whose mirror it is. Along its banks rise white-walled castles and stretch mulberry plantations. On its bosom rise wooded islands, white, but not with frost; for thousands of herons nestle on the branches of the trees, like lilies on their stems. Down under the blue depths, say the people, is the Dragon shrine (Riu Gu), where dwell the dragon-helmed Kai Riu O, and his consort, the shell-crowned Queen of the World Under the Sea.

Why do the pilgrims from all over the empire exclaim joyfully, while climbing Fuji's cinder-beds and lava-blocks, "I am a man of Omi"? Why, when quenching their thirst with the melted snow-water of Fuji crater, do they cry out "I am drinking from Lake Biwa"? Why do the children clap their hands, as they row or sail over Biwa's blue surface, and say: "I am on top of Fuji Yama"?

To these questions the Japanese legend gives answer.

When Heaven and earth were first created, there was neither Lake of Biwa nor Mountain of Fuji. Suruga and Omi were both plains. Even for long after men inhabited Japan and the Mikados had ruled for centuries there was neither earth so nigh to heaven nor water so close to the Underworld as the peaks of Fuji and the bottom of Biwa. Men drove the plow and planted the rice over the very spot where crater and deepest depth now are.

But one night in the ancient times there was a terrible earthquake. All the world shook, the clouds lowered to the earth, floods of water poured from the sky, and a sound like the fighting of a myriad of dragons filled the air. In the morning all was serene and calm. The sky was blue. The earth was as bright and all was as "white-faced" as when the sun goddess first came out from her hiding in the cave.

The people of Omi awoke, scarce expecting to find either earth or heaven, when lo! they looked on what had yesterday been tilled land or barren moor, and there was a great sheet of blue. Was it sky? Had a sheet of the "blue field of heaven" fallen down? Was it the ocean? They came near it, tasted it. It was fresh and sweet as a fountain-rill. They looked at it from the hill-tops, and, seeing its outline, called it "the lake of the four-stringed lute." Others, proud of their new possession, named it the Lake of Omi.

Greater still was the surprise of the Suruga people. The sailors, far out at sea, rubbed their eyes and wondered at the strange shape of the towering white cloud. Was it the Iwakura, the eternal throne of Heaven, come down to rest on earth out of the many piled white clouds of heaven? Some thought they had lost their reckoning; but were assured when they recognized familiar landmarks on shore. Many a cottager woke up to find his house, which lay in a valley the day before, was now far up on the slope, with the distant villages and the sea visible; while far, far above shone the snowy head of a mountain, whose crown lay in the blue sky. At night the edges of the peak, like white fingers, seemed to pluck the stars from the Milky Way.

"What shall we call this new-born child of the gods?" said the people. And various names were proposed.

"There is no other mountain so beautiful in all the earth, there's not its equal anywhere; therefore call it Fuji, (no two such), the peerless, the matchless mountain," said one.

"It is so tall, so comely, so grand, call it Fuji, (rich scholar, the lordly mountain)," said another.

"Call it Fuji, (never dying, the immortal mountain)," said a third.

"Call it, after the festal flower of joy, Fuji" (Wistaria) said another, as he decked the peak of his hat with the drooping clusters of the tender blue blossom. "It looks blue and purple in the distance, just like the fuji flower." Various as the meanings of the name were, they sounded all alike to the ear. So, without any quarreling, all agreed to call it Fuji and each to choose his own meaning. To this day, though many a learned dispute and the scratching of the written character on the sand with walking stick, or on paper with pencil, or on the palm of the hand with forefinger takes place, all pronounce the name alike as they rave on the beauties of Fuji Yama.

So went forth into the countries bounding "the four seas" the belief that there was a white mountain of perfect form in Japan, and that whoever ascended it would live long and even attain immortality; and that somewhere on the mountain was hidden the elixir of immortality, which if any one drank he would live forever. Now in one of the kingdoms of far-off China there lived a rich old king, who had abundance of treasures, health, and many children. But he did not wish to die, and, hence, spent his days in studying the lore and arts of the alchemists, who believed they would finally attain to the transmutation of lead into gold, find the universal solvent of all things, the philosophers' stone, the elixir of life, and all the wondrous secrets which men in Europe long afterward labored to discover.

Among the king's sages was one old man of mighty wisdom, who had heard of the immortal mountain of Japan, and, learning of the manner of its appearance, concluded that the Japan Archipelago contained the Fortunate Isles and in it was the true elixir of life. He divulged his secret to the king, and advised him to make the journey to the Land of the Rising Sun.

Overjoyed at the good news and the faithfulness of his loyal sage, the king loaded him with gifts and honors. He selected five hundred of the most beauteous youths and virgins of his kingdom, and, fitting out a fleet, sailed away to the Happy Isles of the East. Coasting along the shore until they recognized the glorious form of the mountain, they landed and began the ascent. Alas! for the poor king. The rough sea and severe storms had worn on his aged frame and the fatigues of the ascent were so great, that before reaching the top he fainted away, and before the head of the procession had set foot on the crater edge the monarch was dead. Sadly they gave up the search for the elixir of life, and, descending the mountain, buried their master in the Province of Kii. Then, in their exuberance of youth and joy, thinking little of the far future and wishing to enjoy the present, they separated in couples, married, and, disposing of their ship and cargo, settled in the country, and colonized the eastern part of Japan.

Long afterward, when Buddhist believers came to Japan, one of them, climbing Fuji, noticed that around its sunken crater were eight peaks, like the petals of their sacred lotus flower. Thus, it seemed to them, Great Buddha had honored Japan, by bestowing the sacred symbol of Nirvana, or Heaven, on the proudest and highest part of Japan. So they also named it Fuji, "the sacred mountain"; and to this day all the world calls this sacred mountain Fuji, or Fusi Yama, while the Japanese people believe that the earth which sunk in Omi is the same which, piled to the clouds, is the lordly mountain of Suruga.

THE WATERFALL OF YORO, OR THE FOUNTAIN OF YOUTH.

L
LONG, LONG, AGO, when the oldest stork was young, there lived an aged woodcutter and his son on the slopes of the mountain Tagi, in the province of Mino. They gained a frugal livelihood by cutting brushwood on the hill-side, and carrying it in bundles on their back to sell in the nearest market town; for they were too poor to own an ox. With the money thus received they bought rice and radishes, their daily food.

Only once or twice a year, at New Year's and on the mikado's birthday, could they afford to treat themselves to a mess of bean-curd or fresh fish. Yet the old man was very fond of rice-wine, and every week bought a gourd full to keep his old blood warm.

As the years rolled on the aged father's limbs became so stiff that he was unable any longer to climb the mountains. So his son, now grown to be a sturdy man, cut nearly double the quantity of wood and thus kept the family larder full. The old man was so proud of his son that he daily stood at sunset in front of his rustic gate to welcome him back. And to see the old daddy and the young stripling remove their headkerchiefs, and bow with hands on knees in polite fashion, bending their backs and sucking in their breath, out of respect to each other, and to hear them inquiring after one another's health, showering mutual compliments all the time, one would have thought they had not seen each other for eight years, instead of eight hours.

One winter the snow fell long and thick, until all the ground in field and forest was covered several feet over. The bamboo branches bent with their weight of white, the pine boughs broke under their load, and even the stone idols along the wayside were covered up. At first, even with the hardest work, the young woodcutter could scarcely get and sell wood to buy enough food to keep them both alive. He often went hungry himself, so that his father might have his warm wine.

One day he went by another path up one of the mountain dells with his rope basket strapped to his back, and the empty gourd-bottle at his belt. While gloomily grieving over his hard luck, the faint odor of rice-wine seemed borne on the breeze.

He snuffed the air. It was no mistake. "Here's luck, surely," said he, throwing down his bundle.

Hurrying forward he saw a foaming waterfall tumbling over the rocks in a thick stream.

As he drew near, some of the spray fell on his tongue. He tasted it, smacked his lips and throwing down his cord and basket to the ground, filled his gourd and hastened home to his father.

Every day, till the end of his father's life, did he come to this wonderful cascade of wine, and thus the old man was nourished for many a long year.

The news of this fountain of youth spread abroad until it reached the court. The mikado, hearing of it, made a journey to Mino to see the wonderful waterfall. In honor of this event, and as a reward of filial piety, the name of the year-period was changed to Yoro, (Nourishing Old Age).

To this day, many people young and old go out to enjoy picnic parties at the foot of the waterfall; which now, however, runs honest water only, which makes the cheeks red; and not the wonderful wine that once tipped the old daddy's nose with perpetual vermilion.

THE EARTHQUAKE FISH.

MUKASHI, MUKASHI, (as most Japanese stories begin), long, long ago, when the gods came down from heaven to subdue the earth for the mikados, and civilize the country, there were a great many earthquakes, and nothing to stop them. The world continually rocked, and men's houses and lives were never safe.

Now the two gods who were charged with the work of subduing the northeastern part of the world were Kashima and Katori. Having done their work well, and quieted all the enemies of the Sun-goddess, they came to the province of Hitachi. Kashima, sticking his sword into the earth, ran it through to the other side, leaving the hilt above the ground. In the course of centuries this mighty sword shrunk and turned to stone, and the people gave it the name of Kanamé ishi, (The rock of Kanamé).

Now Kanamé means the rivet in a fan, that holds all the sticks together, and they gave the name "rivet-rock," because it is the rivet that binds the earth together. No one could ever lift this rock except Kashima the mighty one who first set it in the earth.

Yet even Kashima never raises it, except to stop an earthquake of unusual violence. When the earth quivers, it is because the great earthquake-fish or jishin-uwo is restless or angry. This jishin-uwo is a great creature something like a catfish. It is about seven hundred miles long, and holds the world on its back. Its tail is at Awomori in the north, and the base of its head is at Kioto, so that all Japan lies on top of it. To his mouth are attached huge twirling feelers, which are just like the hideous moustaches which the hairy-faced men from beyond the Tai-kai (Pacific Ocean) wear on their lips. As soon as these begin to move, it is a sign that the monster is in wrath. When he gets angry, and flaps his tail or bumps his head, there is an earthquake. When he flounders about or rolls over, there is terrible destruction of life and property on the surface of the earth above.

In order to keep the earthquake-fish quiet, the great giant Kashima is appointed to watch him. His business is to stand near by, and when the monster becomes violent Kashima must jump up and straddle him, and hold his gills, put his foot on his fin; and when necessary lift up the great rock of Kanamé and hold him down with its weight. Then he becomes perfectly quiet, and the earthquake ceases. Hence the people sing this earthquake verse:

"No monster can move the Kanamé rock
Though he tug at it never so hard,
For over it stands, resisting the shock,
The Kashima Kami on guard."

Another verse they sing as follows:
"These are things
An earthquake brings;
At nine of the bell they sickness fortell,
At five and seven betoken rain,

At four the sky is cleared thereby,
At six and eight comes wind again."

THE DREAM STORY OF GOJIRO.

O

ONLY a few years ago there was a gentleman in Fukui, Japan, who had a son, a bright lad of twelve, who was very diligent at school and had made astonishing progress in his studies. He was especially quick at learning Chinese characters, of which every Japanese gentleman who wishes to be called educated must know at least two thousand. For, although the Chinese and Japanese are two very different languages, yet the Japanese, Coreans and Chinese use the same letters to write with, just as English, Germans, French and Spaniards all employ one and the same alphabet.

Now Gojiro's father had promised him that when he read through five volumes of the Nihongi, or Ancient History of Japan, he would give him for a present a book of wonderful Chinese stories. Gojiro performed his task, and his father kept his promise. One day on his return from a journey to Kioto, he presented his son with sixteen volumes, all neatly silk-bound, well illustrated with wood-cuts, and printed clearly on thin, silky mulberry paper, from the best wooden blocks. It will be remembered that several volumes of Japanese literature make but one of ours, as they are much lighter and thinner than ours.

Gojiro was so delighted with the wonderful stories of heroes and warriors, travelers and sailors, that he almost felt himself in China. He read far into the night, with the lamp inside of his musquito curtain; and finally fell asleep, still undressed, but with his head full of all sorts of Chinese wonders.

He dreamed he was far away in China, walking along the banks of the great Yellow River. Everything was very strange. The people talked an entirely different language from his own; had on different clothes; and, instead of the nice shaven head and top-knot of the Japanese, every one wore a long pigtail of hair, that dangled at his heels. Even the boats were of a strange form, and on the fishing smacks perched on projecting rails, sat rows of cormorants, each with a ring around his neck. Every few minutes one of them would dive under the water, and after a while come struggling up with a fish in its mouth, so big that the fishermen had to help the bird into the boat. The game was then flung into a basket, and the cormorant was treated to a slice of raw fish, by way of encouragement and to keep the bird from the bad habit of eating the live fish whole. This the ravenous bird would sometimes try to do, even though the ring was put around his neck for the express purpose of preventing him from gulping down a whole fish at once.

It was springtime, and the buds were just bursting into flower. The river was full of fish, especially of carp, ascending to the great rapids or cascades. Here the current ran at a prodigious rate of swiftness, and the waters rippled and boiled and roared with frightful noise. Yet, strange to say, many of the fish were swimming up the stream as if their lives depended on it. They leaped and floundered about; but every one seemed to be tossed back and left exhausted in the river, where they panted and gasped for breath in the eddies at the side. Some were so bruised against the rocks that, after a few spasms, they floated white and stiff, belly up, on the water, dead, and were swept down the stream. Still the shoal leaped and strained every fin, until their scales flashed in the sun like a host of armored warriors in battle. Gojiro, enjoying it as if it were a real conflict of wave and fishes, clapped his hands with delight.

Then Gojiro inquired, by means of writing, of an old white-bearded sage standing by and looking on: "What is the name of this part of the river?"

"We call it Lung Men," said the sage.

"Will you please write the characters for it," said Gojiro, producing his ink-case and brush-pen, with a roll of soft mulberry paper.

The sage wrote the two Chinese characters, meaning "The Gate of the Dragons," or "Dragons' Gate," and turned away to watch a carp that seemed almost up into smooth water.

"Oh! I see," said Gojiro to himself. "That's pronounced Riu Mon in Japanese. I'll go further on and see. There must be some meaning in this fish-climbing." He went forward a few rods, to where the banks trended upward into high bluffs, crowned by towering firs, through the top branches of which fleecy white clouds sailed slowly along, so near the sky did the tree-tops seem. Down under the cliffs the river ran perfectly smooth, almost like a mirror, and broadened out to the opposite shore. Far back, along the current, he could still see the rapids shelving down. It was crowded at the bottom with leaping fish, whose numbers gradually thinned out toward the center; while near the top, close to the edge of level water, one solitary fish, of powerful fin and tail, breasted the steep stream. Now forward a leap, then a slide backward, sometimes further to the rear than the next leap made up for, then steady progress, then a slip, but every moment nearer, until, clearing foam and ripple and spray at one bound, it passed the edge and swam happily in smooth water.

It was inside the Dragon Gate.

Now came the wonderful change. One of the fleecy white clouds suddenly left the host in the deep blue above, dipped down from the sky, and swirling round and round as if it were a water spout, scratched and frayed the edge of the water like a fisher's troll. The carp saw and darted toward it. In a moment the fish was transformed into a white dragon, and, rising into the cloud, floated off toward Heaven. A streak or two of red fire, a gleam of terrible eyes, and the flash of white scales was all that Gojiro saw. Then he awoke.

"How strange that a poor little carp, a common fish that lives in the river, should become a great white dragon, and soar up into the sky, to live there," thought Gojiro, the next day, as he told his mother of his dream.

"Yes," said she; "and what a lesson for you. See how the carp persevered, leaping over all difficulties, never giving up till it became a dragon. I hope my son will mount over all obstacles, and rise to honor and to high office under the government."

"Oh! oh! now I see!" said Gojiro. "That is what my teacher means when he says the students in Tokio have a saying, 'I'm a fish to day, but I hope to be a dragon to-morrow,' when they go to attend examination; and that's what Papa meant when he said: 'That fish's son, Kofuku, has become a white dragon, while I am yet only a carp.'"

THE ASCENT OF THE DRAGON'S GATE.
THE ASCENT OF THE DRAGON'S GATE.

So on the third day of the third month, at the Feast of Flags, Gojiro hoisted the nobori. It was a great fish, made of paper, fifteen feet long and hollow like a bag. It was yellow, with black scales and streaks of gold, and red gills and mouth, in which two strong strings were fastened. It was hoisted up by a rope to the top of a high bamboo pole on the roof of the house. There the breeze caught it, swelled it out round and full of air. The wind made the fins work, and the tail flap, and the head tug, until it looked just like a carp trying to swim the rapids of the Yellow River—the symbol of ambition and perseverance.

THE PROCESSION OF LORD LONG-LEGS.

L

LOVELY AND BRIGHT in the month of May, at the time of rice-planting, was the day on which the daimio, Lord Long-legs, was informed by his chamberlain, Hop-hop, that on the morrow his lordship's retinue would be in readiness to accompany their worshipful Lord Long-legs on his journey. This Lord Long-legs was a daimio who ruled over four acres of rice-field in Echizen, whose revenue was ten thousand rice-stalks. His retainers, who were all grasshoppers, numbered over six thousand, while his court consisted only of nobles, such as Mantis, Beetle, and Pinching-bug. The maids of honor who waited on his queen Katydid, were lady-bugs, butterflies, and goldsmiths, and his messengers were fire-flies and dragon-flies. Once in a while a beetle was sent on an errand; but these stupid fellows had such a habit of running plump into things, and bumping their heads so badly that they always forgot what they were sent for. Besides these, he had a great many servants in the kitchen—such as grubs, spiders, toads, etc. The entire population of his dominion, including the common folks, numbered several millions, and ranked all the way from horse-flies down to ants, mosquitoes, and ticks.

Many of his subjects were very industrious and produced fine fabrics, which, however, were seized and made use of by great monsters, called men. Thus the gray worms kept spinning-wheels in their heads. They had a fashion of eating mulberry leaves, and changing them into fine threads, called silk. The wasps made paper, and the bees distilled honey. There was another insect which spread white wax on the trees. These were all retainers or friendly vassals of Lord Long-legs.

Now it was Lord Long-legs' duty once a year to go up to Yedo to pay his respects to the great Tycoon and to spend several weeks in the Eastern metropolis. I shall not take the time nor tax the patience of my readers in telling about all the bustle and preparation that went on in the yashiki (mansion) of Lord Long-legs for a whole week previous to starting. Suffice it to say that clothes were washed and starched, and dried on a board, to keep them from shrinking; trunks and baskets were packed; banners and umbrellas were put in order; the lacquer on the brass ornaments; shields and swords and spears were all polished; and every little item was personally examined by the daimio's chief inspector. This functionary was a black-and-white-legged mosquito, who, on account of his long nose, could pry into a thing further and see it easier than any other of his lordship's officers; and, if anything went wrong, he could make more noise over it than any one else. As for the retainers, down to the very last lackey and coolie, each one tried to outshine the other in cleanliness and spruce dress.

The Bumble-bee brushed off the pollen from his legs; and the humbler Honey-bee, after allowing his children to suck his paws, to get the honey sticking to them, spruced up and listened attentively to the orders read to him by the train-leader, Sir Locust, who prided himself on being seventeen years old, and looked on all the others as children. He read from a piece of wasp-nest paper: "No leaving the line to suck flowers, except at halting-time." The Blue-tailed Fly washed his hands and face over and over again. The lady-bugs wept many tears, because they could not go with the company; the crickets chirped rather gloomily, because none with short limbs could go on the journey; while Daddy Long-legs almost turned a somersault for joy when told he might carry a bundle in the train. All being in readiness, the procession was to start at six o'clock in the morning. The exact minute was to be announced by the time-keeper of the mansion, Flea san, whose house was on the back of Neko, a great black cat, who lived in the porter's lodge of the castle, near by. Flea san was to notice the opening or slits in the monster's moony-green eyes, which when closed to a certain width would indicate six o'clock. Then with a few jumps she was to announce it to a mosquito friend of hers, who would fly with the news to the gate-keeper of the yashiki, one Whirligig by name.

So, punctually to the hour, the great double gate swung wide open, and the procession passed out and marched on over the hill. All the servants of Lord Long-legs were out, to see the grand sight. They were down on their knees, saying: "O shidzukani," (please go slowly). When their master's palanquin passed, they bowed their heads to the dust, as was proper. The ladies, who were left behind, cried bitterly, and soaked their paper handkerchiefs with tears, especially one fair brown creature, who was next of kin to Lord Long-legs, being an ant on his mother's side.

The procession was closed by six old daddies (spiders), marching two by two, who were a little stupid and groggy, having had a late supper, and a jolly feast the night before. When the great gate slammed shut, one of them caught the end of his foot in it, and was lamed for the rest of the journey. This old Daddy Long-legs, hobbling along, with a bundle on his back, was the only funny thing in the procession, and made much talk among bystanders on the road.

This is the order and the way they looked. First there went out, far ahead, a plump, tall Mantis, with a great long baton of grass, which he swung to and fro before him, from right to left, (like a drum-major), crying out: "Shitaniro, down on your knees! Get down with you!" Whereat all the ants, bugs and lizards at once bent their forelegs, and the toads, which were already squatting, bobbed their noses in the dust. Even the mud-turtles poked their heads out of the water to see what was going on. All the worms and grubs who lived up in trees or tall bushes had to come down to the ground. It was forbidden to any insect to remain on a high stalk of grass, lest he might look down on His Highness. Even the Inch-worm had to wind himself up and stop measuring his length, while the line was passing. And in case of grubs or moths in the nest or cocoon, too young to crawl out, the law compelled their parents to cover them over with a leaf. It would be an insult to Lord Long-legs to look down on him. Next followed two lantern-bearers, holding glow-worms for lanterns in their fore-paws. These were wrapped in cases made of leaves, which they took off at night. Behind were six fire-flies, well supplied with self-acting lamps, which they kept hidden somewhere under their wings. Next marched four abreast the band of little weevils, carrying the umbrellas of state, which were morning-glories—some open, some shut. Behind them strutted four green grasshoppers, who were spear-bearers, carrying pink blossoms. Just before the palanquin were two tall dandies, high lords themselves and of gigantic stature and imposing bellies, who, with arms akimbo and feelers far up in the air, bore aloft high over all the insignia of their Lord Long-legs. All these fellows strutted along on their hind legs, their backs as stiff as a hemp stalk, their noses pointing to the stars, and their legs striding like stilts. The priest in his robes, a praying beetle, who was chaplain, walked on solemnly.

Meanwhile a great crowd of spectators lined the path; but all were on their knees. Frogs and toads blinked out of the sides of their heads. The pretty red lizards glided out, to see the splendid show; worms stopped crawling; and all kinds of bugs ceased climbing, and came down from the grass and flower-stalks, to bow humbly before the train of Lord Long-legs. Bug mothers hastened, with their bug babies on their backs, down to the road, and, squatting down, taught their little nits to put their fore-paws politely together and bow down on their front knees. No one dared to speak out loud; but the mole-cricket, nudging his fellow under the wing, said: "Just look at that green Mantis! He looks as though 'he would rush out with a battle-ax on his shoulder to meet a chariot.' See how he ogles his fellow!"

"Yes; and just behold that bandy-legged hopper, will you? I could walk better than that myself," said the other.

"'Sh!" said the mole-cricket. "Here comes the palanquin."

Everybody now cast a squint up under their eyebrows, and watched the palanquin go by. It was made of delicately-woven striped grass, bound with bamboo threads, lacquered, and finished with curtains of gauze, made of dragon-fly wings, through which Lord Long-legs could peep. It was borne on the shoulders of four stalwart hoppers, who, carrying rest-poles of grass, trudged along, with much sweat and fuss and wiping of their foreheads, stopping occasionally to change shoulders. At their side walked a body-guard of eight hoppers, armed with pistils, and having side-arms of sword-grass. They were also provided with poison-shoots, in case of trouble. Other bearers followed, keeping step and carrying the regalia, consisting of chrysanthemum stalks and blossoms. Then followed, in double rank, a long string of wasps, who were for show and nothing more. Between them, inside, carefully saddled, bridled, and in full housings, was a horse-fly, led by a snail, to keep the restive animal from going at a too rapid pace.

Three big, gawky helmet-headed beetles next followed, bearing rice-sprouts, with full heads of rice.

"Oh! oh! look there!" cried a little grub at the side of the road. "See the little grasshopper riding on his father's back!"

"Hai," said Mother Butterfly, putting one paw on her baby's neck, for fear of being arrested for making a noise.

It was so. The little 'hopper, tired of long walking, had climbed on his father's back for a ride, holding on by the feelers and seeing everything.

Finally, toward the end of the procession, was a great crowd of common 'hoppers, beetles, and bugs of all sorts, carrying the presents to be given in Yedo, and the clothing, food and utensils for the use of Lord Long-legs on the journey; for the hotels were sometimes very poor on the Tokaido high road, and the daimio liked his comforts. Besides, it was necessary for Lord Long-legs to travel with proper dignity, as became a daimio. His messengers always went before and engaged lodging-places, as the fleas, spiders and mosquitoes from other localities, who traveled up and down the great high road, sometimes occupied the places first. The procession wound up by the rear-guard of Daddy Long-legs, who prevented any insult or disrespect from the rabble.

After the line had passed, insects could cross the road, traffic and travel were resumed, and the road was cleared, while the procession faded from view in the distance.

KIYOHIME, OR THE POWER OF LOVE.

Q

QUIET AND SHADY was the spot in the midst of one of the loveliest valley landscapes in the empire, near the banks of the Hidaka river, where stood the tea-house kept by one Kojima. It was surrounded on all sides by glorious mountains, ever robed with deep forests, silver-threaded with flashing water-falls, to which the lovers of nature paid many a visit, and in which poets were inspired to write stanzas in praise of the white foam and the twinkling streamlets. Here the bonzes loved to muse and meditate, and anon merry picnic parties spread their mats, looped their canvas screens, and feasted out of nests of lacquered boxes, drinking the amber saké from cups no larger nor thicker than an egg-shell, while the sound of guitar and drum kept time to dance and song.

The garden of the tea-house was as lovely a piece of art as the florist's cunning could produce. Those who emerged from the deep woods of the lofty hill called the Dragon's Claw, could see in the tea-house garden a living copy of the landscape before them. There were mimic mountains, (ten feet high), and miniature hills veined by a tiny, path with dwarfed pine groves, and tiny bamboo clumps, and a patch of grass for meadow, and a valley just like the great gully of the mountains, only a thousand times smaller, and but twenty feet long. So perfect was the imitation that even the miniature irrigated rice-fields, each no larger than a checker-board, were in full sprout. To make this little gem of nature in art complete, there fell from over a rock at one end a lovely little waterfall two feet high, which after an angry splash over the stones, rolled on over an absurdly small beech, all white-sanded and pebbled, threading its silver way beyond, until lost in fringes of lilies and aquatic plants. In one broad space imitating a lake, was a lotus pond, lined with iris, in which the fins of gold fish and silver carp flashed in the sunbeams. Here and there the nose of a tortoise protruded, while on a rugged rock sat an old grandfather surveying the scene with one or two of his grand-children asleep on his shell and sunning themselves.

The fame of the tea-house, its excellent fare, and special delicacy of its mountain trout, sugar-jelly and well-flavored rice-cakes, drew hundreds of visitors, especially poetry-parties, and lovers of grand scenery.

Just across the river, which was visible from the verandah of the tea-house, stood the lofty firs that surrounded the temple of the Tendai Buddhists. Hard by was the pagoda, which painted red peeped between the trees. A long row of paper-windowed and tile-roofed dwellings to the right made up the monastery, in which a snowy eye-browed but rosy-faced old abbot and some twenty bonzes dwelt, all shaven-faced and shaven-pated, in crape robes and straw sandals, their only food being water and vegetables.

Not the least noticeable of the array of stone lanterns, and bronze images with aureoles round their heads, and incense burners and holy water tanks, and dragon spouts, was the belfry, which stood on a stone platform. Under its roof hung the massive bronze bell ten feet high, which, when struck with a suspended log like a trip-hammer, boomed solemnly over the valley and flooded three leagues of space with the melody which died away as sweetly as an infant falling in slumber. This mighty bell was six inches thick and weighed several tons.

In describing the tea-house across the river, the story of its sweetest charm, and of its garden the fairest flower must not be left untold. Kiyo, the host's daughter, was a lovely maiden of but eighteen, as graceful as the bamboo reed swaying in the breeze of a moonlit summer's eve, and as pretty as the blossoms of the cherry-tree. Far and wide floated the fame of Kiyo, like the fragrance of the white lilies of Ibuki, when the wind sweeping down the mountain heights, comes perfume-laden to the traveler.

As she busied herself about the garden, or as her white socks slipped over the mat-laid floor, she was the picture of grace itself. When at twilight, with her own hands, she lighted the gay lanterns that hung in festoons along the eaves of the tea-house above the verandah, her bright eyes sparkling, her red petticoats half visible through her semi-transparent crape robe, she made many a young man's heart glow with a strange new feeling, or burn with pangs of jealousy.

Among the priests that often passed by the tea-house on their way to the monastery, were some who were young and handsome.

It was the rule of the monastery that none of the bonzes should drink saké (wine) eat fish or meat, or even stop at the tea-houses to talk with women. But one young bonze named "Lift-the-Kettle" (after a passage in the Sanscrit classics) had rigidly kept the rules. Fish had never passed his mouth; and as for saké, he did not know even its taste. He was very studious and diligent. Every day he learned ten new Chinese characters. He had already read several of the sacred sutras, had made a good beginning in Sanskrit, knew the name of every idol in the temple of the 3,333 images in Kioto, had twice visited the sacred shrine of the Capital, and had uttered the prayer "Namu miō ho ren gé kiō," ("Glory be to the sacred lotus of the law"), counting it on his rosary, five hundred thousand times. For sanctity and learning he had no peer among the young neophytes of the bonzerie.

Alas for "Lift-the-Kettle!". One day, after returning from a visit to a famous shrine in the Kuanto, (Eastern Japan), as he was passing the tea-house, he caught sight of Kiyohimé, (the "lady" or "princess" Kiyo), and from that moment his pain of heart began. He returned to his bed of mats, but not to sleep. For days he tried to stifle his passion, but his heart only smouldered away like an incense-stick.

Before many days he made a pretext for again passing the house. Hopelessly in love, without waiting many days he stopped and entered the tea-house.

His call for refreshments was answered by Kiyohimé herself!

As fire kindles fire, so priest and maiden were now consumed in one flame of love. To shorten a long story, "Lift-the-Kettle" visited the inn oftener and oftener, even stealing out at night to cross the river and spend the silent hours with his love.

So passed several months, when suddenly a change come over the young bonze. His conscience began to trouble him for breaking his vows. In the terrible conflict between principle and passion, the soul of the priest was tossed to and fro like the feathered seed-ball of a shuttlecock.

But conscience was the stronger, and won.

He resolved to drown his love and break off his connection with the girl. To do it suddenly, would bring grief to her and a scandal both on her family and the monastery. He must do it gradually to succeed at all.

Ah! how quickly does the sensitive love-plant know the finger-tip touch of cooling passion! How quickly falls the silver column in the crystal tube, at the first breath of the heart's chill even though the words on the lip are warm! Kiyohimé marked the ebbing tide of her lover's regard, and then a terrible resolve of evil took possession of her soul. From that time forth, she ceased to be a pure and innocent and gentle virgin. Though still in maiden form and guise, she was at heart a fox, and as to her nature she might as well have worn the bushy tail of the sly deceiver. She resolved to win over her lover, by her importunities, and failing in this, to destroy him by sorcery.

One night she sat up until two o'clock in the morning, and then, arrayed only in a white robe, she went out to a secluded part of the mountain where in a lonely shrine stood a hideous scowling image of Fudo, who holds the sword of vengeance and sits clothed in fire. There she called upon the god to change her lover's heart or else destroy him.

Thence, with her head shaking, and eyes glittering with anger like the orbs of a serpent, she hastened to the shrine of Kampira, whose servants are the long-nosed sprites, who have the power of magic and of teaching sorcery. Standing in front of the portal she saw it hung with votive tablets, locks of hair, teeth, various tokens of vows, pledges and marks of sacrifice, which the devotees of the god had hung up. There, in the cold night air she asked for the power of sorcery, that she might be able at will to transform herself into the terrible ja,—the awful dragon-serpent whose engine coils are able to crack bones, crush rocks, melt iron or root up trees, and which are long enough to wind round a mountain.

It would be too long to tell how this once pure and happy maiden, now turned to an avenging demon went out nightly on the lonely mountains to practice the arts of sorcery. The mountain-sprites were her teachers, and she learned so diligently that the chief goblin at last told her she would be able, without fail, to transform herself when she wished.

The dreadful moment was soon to come. The visits of the once lover-priest gradually became fewer and fewer, and were no longer tender hours of love, but were on his part formal interviews, while Kiyohimé became more importunate than ever. Tears and pleadings were alike useless, and finally one night as he was taking leave, the bonze told the maid that he had paid his last visit. Kiyohimé then utterly forgetting all womanly delicacy, became so urgent that the bonze tore himself away and fled across the river. He had seen the terrible gleam in the maiden's eyes, and now terribly frightened, hid himself under the great temple bell.

Forthwith Kiyohimé, seeing the awful moment had come, pronounced the spell of incantation taught her by the mountain spirit, and raised her T-shaped wand. In a moment her fair head and lovely face, body, limbs and feet lengthened out, disappeared, or became demon-like, and a fire-darting, hissing-tongued serpent, with eyes like moons trailed over the ground towards the temple, swam the river, and scenting out the track of the fugitive, entered the belfry, cracking the supporting columns made of whole tree-trunks into a mass of ruins, while the bell fell to the earth with the cowering victim inside.

Then began the winding of the terrible coils round and round the metal, as with her wand of sorcery in her hands, she mounted the bell. The glistening scales, hard as iron, struck off sparks as the pressure increased. Tighter and tighter they were drawn, till the heat of the friction consumed the timbers and made the metal glow hot like fire.

THE SORCERESS MELTING THE BELL.

THE SORCERESS MELTING THE BELL.

Vain was the prayer of priest, or spell of rosary, as the bonzes piteously besought great Buddha to destroy the demon. Hotter and hotter grew the mass, until the ponderous metal melted down into a hissing pool of scintillating molten bronze; and soon, man within and serpent without, timber and tiles and ropes were nought but a few handfuls of white ashes.

THE FISHERMAN AND THE MOON-MAIDEN.

P

PEARLY and lustrous white, like a cloud in the far-off blue sky, seemed the floating figure of the moon-maiden, as she flew to earth. She was one of the fifteen glistening virgins that wait attendant upon the moon in her chambers in the sky. Looking down from her high home to the earth, she became enraptured with the glorious scenery of Suruga's ocean shore, and longed for a bath in the blue waters of the sea.

So this fairy maid sped to the earth one morning early, when the moon having shone through the night was about to retire for the day. The sun was rising bright and red over the eastern seas, flushing the mountains and purpling the valleys. Out amid the sparkling waves the ships sailed toward the sun, and the fishermen cast their nets.

It was in early spring, when the air was full of the fragrance of plum blossoms, and the zephyrs blew so softly that scarce a bamboo leaf quivered, or a wave lapsed with sound on the silvery shore.

The moon-maiden was so charmed with the scenery of earth, that she longed to linger above it to gaze tranquilly. Floating slowly through the air, she directed her course to the pine groves that fringe the strand near Cape Miwo. Lying at the base of Fuji mountain, whose snowy crown glistens above, fronting the ocean, whose blue plain undulates in liquid glory till it meets the bending sky, the scenery of Miwo is renowned everywhere under the whole heavens, but especially in the land which the mikado's reign blesses with peace.

Full of happiness, the fairy maiden played sweet music from her flute, until the air was full of it, and it sounded to the dweller on earth like the sweet falling of rain drops on the thirsty ground. Her body shed sweet fragrance through the air, and flowers fell from her robes as she passed. Though none saw her form, all wondered.

Arriving over a charming spot on the sea shore, she descended to the strand, and stood at the foot of a pine tree. She laid her musical instrument on a rock near by, and taking off her wings and feathered suit hung them carefully on the pine tree bough. Then she strolled off along the shore to dip her shining feet in the curling waves.

Picking up some shells, she wondered with innocent joy at the rich tints, which seemed more beautiful than any color in the moon-world. With one, a large smooth scallop, she was particularly pleased; for inside one valve was a yellow disc, and on its mate was a white one.

"How strange," said she. "Here is the sun, and there is the moon. I shall call this the Tsuki-hi-kai—'sun and moon shell'," and she put them in her girdle.

It chanced that near the edge of the pine grove, not far away, there dwelt a lone fisherman, who, coming down to the shore, caught a whiff of sweet perfume such as had never before delighted his nostrils. What could it be? The spring zephyrs, blowing from the west, seemed laden with the sweet odor.

Curiosity prompted him to seek the cause. He walked toward the pine tree, and looking up, caught sight of the feathery suit of wings. Oh! how his eyes sparkled. He danced for joy, and taking down the robe carried it to his neighbors. All were delighted, and one old man said that the fairy must herself be near by. He advised the man to seek until he found her.

So with feathered robe in hand the fisherman went out again to the strand, and took his place near the pine tree. He had not waited long before a lovely being, with rose-tinted white skin and of perfect form, appeared.

"Please good sir, give me back my feathered robe," said she, in a sad voice of liquid sweetness, though she seemed greatly frightened.

"No, I must keep it as a sacred treasure, a relic from a heavenly visitor, and dedicate it in the shrine yonder as a memorial of an angel's visit" said the fisherman.

"Oh, wicked man, what a wretched and impious thing to rob an inhabitant of heaven of the robe by which she moves. How can I fly back to my home again?"

"Give me your wings, oh ye wild geese that fly across the face of the moon, and on tireless pinions seek the icy shores in spring time, and soar unwearied homeward in autumn. Lend me your wings."

But the wild geese overhead only whirred and screamed, and bit their sprays of pine which they carried in their mouth.

"Oh, ye circling gulls, lend me but for a day your downy wings. I am prisoner here", cried the weeping fairy.

But the graceful gulls hovering for a moment swept on in widening circles out to farther sea.

"Oh, breezes of the air which blow whither ye list! Oh, tide of ocean which ebbs and flows at will! Ye may move all, but I am prisoner here, devoid of motion. Oh, good sir have pity and give me back my wings," cried the moon-maiden, pressing her hands together in grief.

The fisher's heart was touched by the pathos of her voice and the glittering of her tears.

"I'll give back your winged-robe if you'll dance and make music for me", said he.

"Oh, yes, good sir, I will dance and make music, but first let me put on my feather-robe for without it I have no power of motion."

"Oh, yes", said the suspicious mortal, "If I give you back your wings you'll fly straight to heaven."

"What! can you not believe the word of a heavenly being, without doubting? Trust me in good faith and you'll lose nothing."

Then with shamed face the fisherman handed to the moon-maiden her feathered robe, which she donned and began to dance. She poured out such sweet strains from her upright flute that with eye and ear full of rapture, the fisherman imagined himself in heaven. Then she sang a sweet song in which she described the delights of life in the moon and the pleasure of celestial residence.

The fisherman was so overjoyed that he longed to detain the fairy. He begged her to dwell with him on earth, but in vain. As he looked, he saw her rising. A fresh breeze, rippling the face of the sea, now sprang up, and wafted the pearly maiden over the pine-clad hills and past Fuji mountain. All the time sweet music rained through the air until, as the fisherman strained his eyes toward the fresh-fallen snow on Fuji's crest, he could no longer distinguish the moon-maiden from the fleecy clouds that filled the thin air.

Pondering long upon the marvelous apparition, the fisherman resolved to mark the spot where the fairy first descended to earth. So he prevailed upon the simple villagers to build a railing of stone around the now sacred pine.

Daily they garlanded the old trunk with festoons of tasseled and twisted rice-straw. Long after, when by the storms of centuries the old pine, in spite of bandages and crutches, and tired of wrestling with the blast, fell down like an old man, to rise no more, a grateful posterity cleared the space and built the shrine of Miwo, which still dots with its sacred enclosure the strand of Suruga on which the fairy danced.

THE JEWELS OF THE EBBING AND THE FLOWING TIDE.

CHIUAI was the fourteenth mikado of the Land of the Gods (Japan). His wife, the empress, was named Jingu, or Godlike Exploit. She was a wise and discreet lady and assisted her husband to govern his dominions. When a great rebellion broke out in the south island called Kiushiu, the mikado marched his army against the rebels. The empress went with him and lived in the camp. One night, as she lay asleep in her tent, she dreamed that a heavenly being appeared to her and told her of a wonderful land in the west, full of gold, silver, jewels, silks and precious stones. The heavenly messenger told her if she would invade this country she would succeed, and all its spoil would be hers, for herself and Japan.

"Conquer Corea!" said the radiant being, as she floated away on a purple cloud.

In the morning the empress told her husband of her dream, and advised him to set out to invade the rich land. But he paid no attention of her. When she insisted, in order to satisfy her, he climbed up a high mountain, and looking far away towards the setting sun, saw no land thither, not even mountain peaks. So, believing that there was no country in that direction he descended, and angrily refused to set out on the expedition. Shortly after, in a battle with the rebels the mikado was shot dead with an arrow.

The generals and captains of the host then declared their loyalty to the empress as the sole ruler of Japan. She, now having the power, resolved to carry out her daring plan of invading Corea. She invoked all the kami or gods together, from the mountains, rivers and plains to get their advice and help. All came at her call. The kami of the mountains gave her timber and iron for her ships; the kami of the fields presented rice and grain for provisions; the kami of the grasses gave her hemp for cordage; and the kami of the winds promised to open his bag and let out his breezes to fill her sails toward Corea. All came except Isora, the kami of the sea shore. Again she called for him and sat up waiting all night with torches burning, invoking him to appear.

Now, Isora was a lazy fellow, always slovenly and ill-dressed, and when at last he did come, instead of appearing in state in splendid robes, he rose right out of the sea-bottom, covered with mud and slime, with shells sticking all over him and sea-weed clinging to his hair. He gruffly asked what the empress wanted.

"Go down to Riu Gu and beg his majesty Kai Riu O, the Dragon King of the World Under the Sea, to give me the two jewels of the tides," said the imperial lady.

Now among the treasures in the palace of the Dragon King of the World Under the Sea were two jewels having wondrous power over the tides. They were about as large as apples, but shaped like apricots, with three rings cut near the top. They seemed to be of crystal, and glistened and shot out dazzling rays like fire. Indeed, they appeared to seethe and glow like the eye of a dragon, or the white-hot steel of the sword-forger. One was called the Jewel of the Flood-Tide, and the other the Jewel of the Ebb-Tide. Whoever owned them had the power to make the tides instantly rise or fall at his word, to make the dry land appear, or the sea overwhelm it, in the fillip of a finger.

Isora dived with a dreadful splash, down, down to Riu Gu, and straightway presented himself before Kai Riu O. In the name of the empress, he begged for the two tide-jewels.

The Dragon King agreed, and producing the flaming globes from his casket, placed them on a huge shell and handed them to Isora, who brought the jewels to Jingu, who placed them in her girdle.

The empress now prepared her fleet for Corean invasion. Three thousand barges were built and launched, and two old kami with long streaming gray hair and wrinkled faces, were made admirals. Their names were Suwa Daimiō Jin (Great Illustrious, Spirit of Suwa) and Sumiyoshi Daimiō Jin, the kami who lives under the old pine tree at Takasago, and presides over nuptial ceremonies.

The fleet sailed in the tenth month. The hills of Hizen soon began to sink below the horizon, but no sooner were they out of sight of land than a great storm arose. The ships tossed about, and began to butt each other like bulls, and it seemed as though the fleet would be driven back; when lo! Kai Riu O sent shoals of huge sea-monsters and immense fishes that bore up the ships and pushed their sterns forward with their great snouts. The shachihoko, or dragon-fishes, taking the ship's cables in their mouths towed them forward, until the storm ceased and the ocean was calm. Then they plunged downwards into the sea and disappeared.

The mountains of Corea now rose in sight. Along the shore were gathered the Corean army. Their triangular fringed banners, inscribed with dragons, flapped in the breeze. As soon as their sentinels caught sight of the Japanese fleet, the signal was given, and the Corean line of war galleys moved gaily out to attack the Japanese.

The empress posted her archers in the bows of her ships and waited for the enemy to approach. When they were within a few hundred sword-lengths, she took from her girdle the Jewel of the Ebbing Tide and cast the flashing gem into the sea. It blazed in the air for a moment, but no sooner did it touch the water, than instantly the ocean receded from under the Corean vessels, and left them stranded on dry land. The Coreans, thinking it was a tidal wave, and that the Japanese ships were likewise helpless in the undertow, leaped out of their galleys and rushed over the sand, and on to the attack. With shouting and drawn swords their aspect was terrible. When within range of the arrows, the Japanese bowmen opened volleys of double-headed, or triple-pronged arrows on the Coreans, and killed hundreds.

But on they rushed, until near the Japanese ships, when the empress taking out the Flood-Tide Jewel, cast it in the sea. In a snap of the finger, the ocean rolled up into a wave many tens of feet high and engulfed the Corean army, drowning them almost to a man. Only a few were left out of the ten thousand. The warriors in their iron armor sank dead in the boiling waves, or were cast along the shore like logs. The Japanese army landed safely, and easily conquered the country. The king of Corea surrendered and gave his bales of silk, jewels, mirrors, books, pictures, robes, tiger skins, and treasures of gold and silver to the empress. The booty was loaded on eighty ships, and the Japanese army returned in triumph to their native country.

KAI RIU O, THE DRAGON KING OF THE WORLD UNDER THE SEA.

S
SOON AFTER her arrival at home, the empress Jingu gave birth to a son, whom she named Ojin. He was one of the fairest children ever born of an imperial mother, and was very wise and wonderful even when an infant. He was a great favorite of Takénouchi, the prime minister of the empress. As he grew up, he was full of the Yamato Damashii, or the spirit of unconquerable Japan.

This Takénouchi was a very venerable old man, who was said to be three hundred and sixty years old. He had been the counsellor of five mikados. He was very tall, and as straight as an arrow, when other old men were bent like a bow. He served as a general in war and a civil officer in peace. For this reason he always kept on a suit of armor under his long satin and damask court robes. He wore the bear-skin shoes and the tiger-skin scabbard which were the general's badge of rank, and also the high cap and long fringed strap hanging from the belt, which marked the court noble. He had moustaches, and a long beard fell over his breast like a foaming waterfall, as white as the snows on the branches of the pine trees of Ibuki mountain.

Now the empress, as well as Takénouchi, wished the imperial infant Ojin to live long, be wise and powerful, become a mighty warrior, be invulnerable in battle, and to have control over the tides and the ocean as his mother once had. To do this it was necessary to get back the Tide Jewels.

So Takénouchi took the infant Ojin on his shoulders, mounted the imperial war-barge, whose sails were of gold-embroidered silk, and bade his rowers put out to sea. Then standing upright on the deck, he called on Kai Riu O to come up out of the deep and give back the Tide Jewels to Ojin.

At first there was no sign on the waves that Kai Riu O heard. The green sea lay glassy in the sunlight, and the waves laughed and curled above the sides of the boat. Still Takénouchi listened intently and waited reverently. He was not long in suspense. Looking down far under the sparkling waves, he saw the head and fiery eyes of a dragon mounting upward. Instinctively he clutched his robe with his right hand, and held Ojin tightly on his shoulder, for this time not Isora, but the terrible Kai Riu O himself was coming.

What a great honor! The sea-king's servant, Isora, had appeared to a woman, the empress Jingu, but to her son, the Dragon King of the World Under the Sea deigned to come in person.

The waters opened; the waves rolled up, curled, rolled into wreaths and hooks and drops of foam, which flecked the dark green curves with silvery bells. First appeared a living dragon with fire-darting eyes, long flickering moustaches, glittering scales of green all ruffled, with terrible spines erect, and the joints of the fore-paws curling out jets of red fire. This living creature was the helmet of the Sea King. Next appeared the face of awful majesty and stern mien, as if with reluctant condescension, and then the jewel robes of the monarch. Next rose into view a huge haliotis shell, in which, on a bed of rare gems from the deep sea floor, glistened, blazed and flashed the two Jewels of the Tides.

Then the Dragon-King spoke, saying:

"Quick, take this casket, I deign not to remain long in this upper world of mortals. With these I endow the imperial prince of the Heavenly line of the mikados of the Divine country. He shall be invulnerable in battle. He shall have long life. To him I give power over sea and land. Of this, let these Tide-Jewels be the token."

Hardly were these words uttered when the Dragon-King disappeared with a tremendous splash. Takénouchi standing erect but breathless amid the crowd of rowers who, crouching at the boat's bottom had not dared so much as to lift up their noses, waited a moment, and then gave the command to turn the prow to the shore.

Ojin grew up and became a great warrior, invincible in battle and powerful in peace. He lived to be one hundred and eleven years old, and was next to the last of the long lived mikados of Everlasting Great Japan.

To this day Japanese soldiers honor him as the patron of war, and pray to him as the ruler of battle.

When the Buddhist priests came to Japan they changed his name to Hachiman Dai Bosatsu, or the "Great Buddha of the Eight Banners." On many a hill and in many a village of Japan may still be seen a shrine to his honor. Often when a soldier comes back from war, he will hang up a tablet or picture-frame, on which is carved a painting or picture of the two-edged short sword like that which Ojin carried. Many of the old soldiers who fought in armor wore a little silver sword of Ojin set as a frontlet to their helmets, for a crest of honor. On gilded or lacquered Japanese cabinets and shrines, and printed on their curious old, and new greenback paper money, are seen the blazing Jewels of the Tides. On their gold and silver coins the coiled dragon clutches in his claws the Jewels of the Ebbing and the Flowing Tide. One of the iron-clad war ships of the imperial Japanese navy, on which floats proudly the red sun-banner of the Empire of the Rising Sun, is named Kōgō (Empress) after the Amazon empress who in the third century carried the arms of the Island Empire into the main land of Asia, and won victory by her mastery over the ebbing and the flowing tides.

    THE DRAGON KING'S GIFT OF THE TIDE JEWELS.
THE DRAGON KING'S GIFT OF THE TIDE JEWELS.

THE CREATION OF HEAVEN AND EARTH.

O

OF OLD the Heavens and the Earth were not separated. Land and water, solids and gases, fire and stone, light and darkness were mixed together. All was liquid and turbid chaos.

Then the mighty mass began to move from within. The lighter particles of gas and air began to rise, forming the sky and heavens. The heavy parts sank and cohered, becoming the earth. The water formed the four seas. Then there appeared something like a white cloud floating between heaven and earth. Out of this came forth three beings—The Being of the Middle of Heaven, The High August Being, and The Majestic Being. These three "hid their bodies."

Out of the warm mould of the earth something like a rush sprouted up. It was clear and bright like crystal. From this rush-sprout came forth a being whose title is "The Delightful and Honorable Rush-Sprout." Next appeared another being out of the buds of the rush-sprout whose name is "The Honorable Heaven-born." These five beings are called "the heavenly gods."

Next came into existence four pairs of beings viz.: (1) The Being Sprung from the First Mud, and The Being of the Sand and Mud; (2) The Being with Hands and Feet Growing, and the Being Having Breath; (3) The Male Being, and the Female Being of the Great Place (the earth); (4) The Being of Complete Perfection, and the Being who cried out "Strange and Awful" to her mate.

Thus the last pair that came into existence were the first man and woman called Izanagi and Izanami.

It is said that the other pairs of beings before Izanagi and Izanami were only their imperfect forms or the processes through which they passed before arriving at perfection.

These two beings lived in the Heavens. The world was not yet well formed, and the soil floated about like a fish in the water, but near the surface; and was called "The Floating Region." The sun, earth and moon were still attached to each other like a head to the neck, or arms to the body. They were little by little separating, the parts joining them growing thinner and thinner. This part, like an isthmus, was called "Heaven's Floating Bridge." It was on this bridge that Izanagi and Izanami were standing when they saw a pair of wagtails cooing and billing sweetly together. The heavenly couple were so delighted with the sight that they began to imitate the birds. Thus began the art of love, which mortals have practiced to this day.

While talking together on this Bridge of Heaven, they began to wonder if there was a world beneath them. They looked far down upon the green seas, but could see nothing! Then Izanagi took his long jeweled spear and plunged it into the turbid mass, turning it round and round. As he lifted it up, the drops which trickled from it hardened into earth of their own accord; and thus dry land was formed. As Izanagi was cleansing his spear the lumps of muck and mud which had adhered to it flew off into space, and were changed into stars and comets.

[It is said that by turning his spear round and round, Izanagi set the Earth revolving in daily revolutions].

To the land thus formed, they gave the name of "The Island of the Congealed Drop," because they intended to create a large archipelago and wished to distinguish this as the first island. They descended from Heaven on the floating bridge and landed on the island. Izanagi struck his tall spear in the ground making it the axis of the world. He then proceeded to build a palace around the spear which formed the central pillar. [This spot was formerly at the North pole, but is now at Eshima, off the central eastern coast of Japan]. They then resolved to walk round the island and examine it. This done, they met together. Izanami cried out, "What a lovely man!" But Izanagi rebuked her for speaking first, and said they must try it again. Then they walked round the island once more. When they met, Izanami held her tongue while Izanagi said, "What a lovely woman!"

Being now both in good humor, they began the work of creating Japan. The first island brought up out of the water was Awaji; and then the main island. After that, eight large islands were created, whence comes one of the names of Japan, "The Empire of the Eight Great Islands." Six smaller islands were also produced. The several thousand islets which make up the archipelago of Everlasting Great Japan were formed by the spontaneous consolidation of the foam of the sea.

After the country was thus formed the divine pair created eight millions of earthly gods or kami, and the ten thousand different things on the earth. Vegetation sprang up over all the land, which was however still covered with mist. So Izanagi created with his breath the two gods, male and female of the wind. All these islands are the children of Izanagi and Izanami, and when first born were small and feeble, but gradually grew larger and larger, attaining their present size like human beings, which are at first tiny infants.

As the gradual separation of the land and sea went on, foreign countries were formed by the congealing of the foam of the sea. The god of fire was then born of Izanami, his mother. This god often got very angry at any one who used unclean fire. Izanami then created by herself the gods of metals, of clay and of fresh water. This latter was told always to keep the god of fire quiet, and put him out when he began to do mischief.

Izanagi and Izanami, though married but a short time, began to quarrel, for Izanami had once told her husband not to look at her when she hid herself. But Izanagi did not do what she requested, but intruded on her privacy when she was unwell, and stared at her when she wished to be alone. Izanami then got very angry, and went down to the lower world of darkness, and disappeared.

In the dark world under the earth Izanami stayed a long time, and after long waiting, Izanagi went after her. In the darkness of the Under-world he was horrified at what he saw, and leaving his consort below, tried to escape to the earth again.

In his struggles several gods were created, one of them coming out of his staff. When he got up to daylight, he secured a large rock to close up the hole in the earth. Turning this rock into a god, he commanded him to watch the place. He then rushed into the sea and continued washing for a long time to purify himself. In blowing out from his lungs the polluted air inhaled in the Under-world, the two evil gods sprang forth from his breath. As these would commit great harm and wickedness, Izanagi created two other gods to correct their evil. But when he had washed his eyes and could see clearly again, there sprang out two precious and lovely beings; one from his left eye, being a rare and glistening maiden, whom he afterwards named Ama Térasu, or "The

Heaven Illuminating Spirit." From his right eye appeared Susa no O, the "Ruler of the Moon." Being now pure again, and having these lovely children, Izanagi rejoiced and said, "I have begotten child upon child, and at the end of my begetting, I have begotten me two jewel-children." Now the brightness of the person of the maiden Ama Térasu was beautiful, and shone through Heaven and Earth. Izanagi, well pleased, said: "Though my children are many, none of them is like this wonder-child. She must not be kept in this region." So taking off the necklace of precious stones from his neck and rattling it, he gave it to her, saying, "Rule thou over the High Plain of Heaven."

At that time the distance between Heaven and Earth was not very great, and he sent her up to the blue sky by the Heaven-uniting Pillar, on which the Heavens rested like a prop. She easily mounted it, and lived in the sun, illuminating the whole Heavens and the Earth. The Sun now gradually separated from the Earth, and both moved farther and farther apart until they rested where they now are.

Izanagi next spoke to Susa no O the Ruler of the Moon, and said, "Rule thou over the new-born Earth and the blue Waste of the Sea, with its Multitudinous Salt Waters."

[So then the Heavens and the Earth and Moon were created and inhabited. And as Japan lay directly opposite the sun when it separated from the Earth, it is plain that Japan lies on the summit of the globe. It is easily seen that all other countries were formed by the spontaneous consolidation of the ocean foam, and the collection of mud in the various seas. The stars were made to guide warriors from foreign countries to the court of the Mikado, who is the true Son of Heaven].

HOW THE SUN GODDESS WAS ENTICED OUT OF HER CAVE.

W
WHEN THE far-shining goddess, on account of the evil pranks of her brother, Susa no O, the Ruler of the Moon, hid herself in a cave, there was no more light, and heaven and earth were plunged into darkness.

A council of all the gods was held in the dry bed of one of the rivers [which we call the Milky Way] in the fields of Heaven. The question of how to appease the anger of the goddess was discussed. A long-headed and very wise god was ordered to think out a plan to entice her forth from the cave.

After due deliberation, it was resolved that a looking-glass should be made to tempt her to gaze at herself, and that tricks should be played to arouse her curiosity to come out and see what was going on.

So setting to work with a will, the gods forged and polished a mirror, wove cloth for beautiful garments, built a pavilion, carved a necklace of jewels, made wands, and tried an augury.

All being ready, the fat and rosy-cheeked goddess of mirth with face full of dimples, and eyes full of fun, named Uzumé, was selected to lead the dance. She had a flute made from a bamboo cane by piercing holes between the joints, while every god in the great orchestra had a pair of flat hard wood clappers, which he struck together.

She bound up her long flowing sleeves with a creeper vine, and made for herself a baton of twigs of bamboo grass, by which she could direct the motions of the musicians. This she held in one hand while in the other was a spear wound round with grass, on which small bells tinkled. Great bonfires were lighted in front of the cave, so that the audience of gods could see the dance. A large circular box which resounded like a drum when trod on, was set up for Uzumé to dance upon. The row of cocks now began to crow in concert.

All being ready, the Strong-handed god who was to pull the sun-goddess out of the cave, as soon as overcome by her curiosity she should peep forth, hid himself beside the stone door of the cave. Uzumé mounted the box and began to dance. As the drum-box resounded, the spirit of folly seized her, and she began to chant a song.

Becoming still more foolish, Uzumé waved her wand wildly, loosened her dress, and danced till she had not a stitch of clothing left on her. The gods were so amused at her foolishness that they all laughed, until the heavens shook as with claps of thunder.

The Sun-goddess within the cave heard all these strange noises; the crowing of the cocks, the hammering on the anvil, the chopping of wood, the music of the koto, the clappering of the hard wood, the tinkling of the bells, the shouting of Uzumé and the boisterous laughter of the gods. Wondering what it all meant, she peeped out.

As she did so the Doubly Beautiful goddess held up the mirror.

The Far-Shining one seeing her own face in it was greatly astonished. Curiosity got the better of fear. She looked far out. Instantly the strong-handed god pulled the rocky door open, and seizing her hand, dragged her forth. Then all the heavens and earth were lightened, the trees and grass became green again, and the goddess of colors resumed her work of tinting the flowers. The gloom fled from all eyes, and human beings again became "white-faced."

Thus the calamity which had befallen heaven and earth, by the sun-goddess hiding in the cave became a means of much benefit to mortals. For by their necessity the gods were compelled to invent the arts of metal-working, weaving, carpentry, jeweling and many other useful appliances for the human race. They also on this occasion first made use of music, dancing, the Dai Kagura (The comedy which makes the gods laugh) and many of the games which the children play at the present time.

TRANSCRIBER'S NOTES

Place names and proper names have various spelling throughout the book. These have been left as written in the original book. Apart from those items listed below, all parochial, unusual and non-standard spelling, grammar and punctuation has been left as printed in the original book.

The use of the macron above the letter "O" in names throughout the book is inconsistent. The same name may appear either with or without a macron or the macron may appear above different letters when the same name is printed in different places through the book. This has been left as printed in the original book.